AMERICA'S #1 STANDARDS-BASED SCHOOL IMPROVEMENT

ACT • PLAN • EXPLORE
Science Reasoning Victory
Student Textbook

ACT•PLAN•EXPLORE•SAT•PSAT•SATII•GRE•GMAT•LSAT•MCAT•TOEFL•GED•PRAXIS•PSAE•ITBS•CollegePrep™

Copyright © 2005, 2004 by Cambridge Publishing, Inc.
Published by Cambridge Publishing, Inc.
All rights reserved
including the right of reproduction
in whole or in part in any form.

Cambridge Educational Services, Inc.
2720 River Road, Des Plaines, IL 60018
(847) 299-2930

Portions reprinted from ACT by Thomas H. Martinson.
Copyright © 2005 by Thomas H. Martinson.
All rights reserved
including the right of reproduction
in whole or in part in any form.

Manufactured in the United States of America.
2 3 4 5 6 7 8 9 10

Dear Student,

The fact that you're reading this book means just one thing—you've got a big, important test ahead of you. You want to do well, and we want to help you. This book will enable you not only to succeed on the ACT, PLAN, or EXPLORE, but also to improve your all-around academic performance.

Since you began going to school, you've been taught thousands of things. No one expects you to remember every single concept that you've learned since you were 5 years old. However, the ACT, PLAN, and EXPLORE are cumulative tests, which means that you might be tested on concepts that you may have forgotten or that you may never have learned at all. Not only that, but the ACT, PLAN, and EXPLORE test these concepts in very particular ways that most of your in-school tests never have.

This Cambridge ACT • PLAN • EXPLORE Science Reasoning Student Textbook contains all of the materials that you need in order to: 1) refresh or build your understanding of important Science Reasoning skills; 2) apply those skills in the particular context of the ACT, PLAN, or EXPLORE; and 3) reduce test anxiety through practice.

You've got the tools to succeed. If you attend class, participate in learning, do all of your homework, and maintain a positive attitude, then you will do well.

Good Luck!

The Cambridge Curriculum Committee

ACT • PLAN • EXPLORE
SCIENCE REASONING
Table of Contents

INTRODUCTION
    How to Use This Book 3

STEP ONE: DIAGNOSTIC TESTING AND ASSESSMENT SERVICE
    Cambridge Course Concept Outline—Step One 11
    ACT • PLAN • EXPLORE Diagnostic Pre-Test Student Progress Report 13
    ACT • PLAN • EXPLORE Diagnostic Pre-Test Instructor Progress Report 15
    ACT • PLAN • EXPLORE Pre-Test Bubble Sheet 17

STEP TWO: SKILLS REVIEW
    Cambridge Course Concept Outline—Step Two 23
    ACT • PLAN • EXPLORE Science Reasoning Step Two Student Progress Report 25
    ACT • PLAN • EXPLORE Science Reasoning Step Two Instructor Progress Report 27
    Science Skills Review 31
        Understanding Scientific Information 31
        Basics of Experimental Design 33
            Exercise 1—Basics of Experimental Design 35
        Data Organization in Controlled Experiments 36
            Exercise 2—Data Organization in Controlled Experiments 40
        Presentation of Conflicting Viewpoints 42
            Exercise 3—Presentation of Conflicting Viewpoints 43
        Exercise 4—Science Reasoning Passages 44

STEP THREE: PROBLEM-SOLVING, CONCEPTS, AND STRATEGIES
    Cambridge Course Concept Outline—Step Three 53
    ACT • PLAN • EXPLORE Science Reasoning Step Three Student Progress Report 55
    ACT • PLAN • EXPLORE Science Reasoning Step Three Instructor Progress Report 57
    Section One—Science Reasoning Review 61
    Section Two—Science Reasoning Problem-Solving 76
    Section Three—Science Reasoning Quizzes 94
        Quiz I 94
        Quiz II 96
        Quiz III 98
    Strategy Summary Sheet—Science Reasoning 102

STEP FOUR: PRACTICE TEST REINFORCEMENT
    Cambridge Course Concept Outline—Step Four 109
    ACT Science Reasoning Step Four Student Progress Report 111
    ACT Science Reasoning Step Four Instructor Progress Report 113
    ACT Practice Test Bubble Sheets 115
    ACT Science Reasoning Practice Test I 125
    ACT Science Reasoning Practice Test II 135
    ACT Science Reasoning Practice Test III 145
    ACT Science Reasoning Practice Test IV 157

STEP FIVE: FINAL EXAM, ASSESSMENT REPORT, AND REVIEW
   Cambridge Course Concept Outline—Step Five 171
   ACT • PLAN • EXPLORE Diagnostic Post-Test Student Progress Report 173
   ACT • PLAN • EXPLORE Diagnostic Post-Test Instructor Progress Report..175
   ACT • PLAN • EXPLORE Post-Test Bubble Sheet..177

STEP SIX: PERSONAL STUDY PLAN
   Cambridge Course Concept Outline—Step Six 183
   ACT • PLAN • EXPLORE Science Reasoning Step Six Student Progress Report....................................185
   ACT • PLAN • EXPLORE Science Reasoning Step Six Instructor Progress Report 187
   ACT • PLAN • EXPLORE English Step Six Student Progress Report 189
   ACT • PLAN • EXPLORE English Step Six Instructor Progress Report..191
   ACT • PLAN • EXPLORE Mathematics Step Six Student Progress Report..193
   ACT • PLAN • EXPLORE Mathematics Step Six Instructor Progress Report..195
   ACT • PLAN • EXPLORE Reading Step Six Student Progress Report 197
   ACT • PLAN • EXPLORE Reading Step Six Instructor Progress Report..199

ANSWERS AND EXPLANATIONS
   Step Two: Skills Review..205
      Exercise 1—Basics of Experimental Design...205
      Exercise 2—Data Organization in Controlled Experiments 205
      Exercise 3—Presentation of Conflicting Viewpoints 205
      Exercise 4—Science Reasoning Passages..206
   Step Three: Problem-Solving, Concepts, and Strategies 207
      Section One—Science Reasoning Review..207
      Section Two—Science Reasoning Problem-Solving 207
      Section Three—Science Reasoning Quizzes..207
         Quiz I..207
         Quiz II 207
         Quiz III 207
   Step Four: Practice Test Reinforcement..208
      Practice Test I..208
      Practice Test II...211
      Practice Test III..214
      Practice Test IV 217

ACT • PLAN • EXPLORE
SCIENCE REASONING

INTRODUCTION

HOW TO USE THIS BOOK

This book is organized into six parts:

1) Forms that help you make sense of your official Science Reasoning diagnostic pre-test results (Step One);
2) Science Skills Review (Step Two);
3) Science Reasoning problems resembling those on the real ACT, PLAN, and EXPLORE that your instructor will use to teach tested concepts and applicable strategies (Step Three);
4) Four full-length ACT Science Reasoning Practice Tests (Step Four);
5) Forms that help you make sense of your official Science Reasoning post-test results (Step Five); and
6) Forms that help you determine what to do at the end of your Cambridge course to maximize your ACT, PLAN, or EXPLORE score (Step Six).

The following brief introduction will explain how to effectively use each part of this textbook.

MAKING SENSE OF YOUR OFFICIAL PRE-TEST RESULTS

In order to know where to begin preparing for the ACT, PLAN, or EXPLORE, you first have to know what you already do well and what you could learn to do better. Step One serves this purpose. First, you will take an official, retired ACT, PLAN, or EXPLORE under actual testing conditions. Then, with the help of your instructor, you will use the results of those tests to determine exactly which problems to review, how long to review them, and in what order.

In Step One of this book, you will find a progress report form (p. 13) in which you will record your results for the Science Reasoning portion of the diagnostic pre-test. Recording your results will help you to see your strengths and weaknesses more clearly. In addition, Step One contains a pre-test bubble sheet. You can use this sheet to respond to all areas of the pre-test, not just the Science Reasoning portion. *Use the other portions of this sheet only if your instructor tells you to do so.*

SCIENCE SKILLS REVIEW

The Skills Review (Step Two) contains problems that will enable you to do three things: 1) review material that you may have forgotten; 2) learn material that you may never have learned; and 3) master the skills that you need to answer the more difficult multiple-choice questions on the ACT, PLAN, and EXPLORE. The problems in the Science Skills Review are at or below skill level so that students can use them to build fundamental skills.

Each chapter contains concept lessons and corresponding review exercises. The lessons in the Science Skills Review cover the following topics:

- Basics of Experimental Design
- Data Organization in Controlled Experiments
- Presentation of Conflicting Viewpoints
- Science Reasoning Passages

These exercises do not necessarily contain problems that mimic ACT, PLAN, and EXPLORE problems. They are designed to help you learn concepts—not to necessarily help you learn about a peculiarity of the actual test. After you have mastered the skills, you will be able to take full advantage of the test-taking strategies developed in Step Three of this book. Your instructor may either review the Science Skills Review material in class or have you complete the exercises as homework.

Step Two also contains a progress report form (p. 25). This form lists every exercise in the Science Skills Review, providing a table for you to record how many problems you've completed and what percentage you've answered correctly. After you've completed each exercise, be sure to fill out the respective portion of the progress

INTRODUCTION

report. The form will document your progress and make it easier to recognize exactly what material in Step Three deserves most of your attention.

SOLVING PROBLEMS LIKE THOSE FOUND ON THE TEST

Problem-solving, concepts, and strategies make up the heart of this course and, in particular, this textbook. Step Three contains problems that resemble those on the actual ACT, PLAN, and EXPLORE Science Reasoning sections. When compared to problems on the actual test, the problems in this part of the book have similar content, represent the same difficulty range, and can be solved by using the same problem-solving skills and alternative test-taking strategies.

This part of the book is divided into three sections:

- Section One: Science Reasoning Review
- Section Two: Science Reasoning Problem-Solving
- Section Three: Science Reasoning Quizzes

At the beginning of Step Three, there is a Cambridge Course Concept Outline. The outline acts as a course syllabus and lists the concepts that are tested for each problem-type over a two-year testing cycle. The problems in Section One are organized to correspond with the course concept outline. For each concept in the outline, there are various clusters of problems. A cluster contains a greater number of problems if the problem-type appears more frequently on the real test, and it contains fewer problems if the problem-type appears less frequently. Although the same concept is not tested consecutively on the real ACT, PLAN, and EXPLORE, Cambridge organizes the problems in clusters so that the concepts are emphasized and reinforced. Your instructor will use the Science Reasoning Review problems to teach Science Reasoning concepts and to demonstrate problem-solving techniques and alternative test-taking strategies.

In Section Two, the problems are generally at a higher difficulty level; they give you a chance to apply the problem-solving techniques and alternative strategies that you learned in the Science Reasoning Review. Finally, Section Three introduces the elements of timing and pacing. Once you have mastered the concepts and strategies of the ACT • PLAN • EXPLORE Science Reasoning material in the first two sections, you will be ready to take on the added pressure of time limits in the Science Reasoning Quizzes. The practice tests located in Step Four of this book (p. 107) provide additional opportunities for you to practice applying this conceptual knowledge, both with and without time restrictions.

Step Three also contains a progress report form (p. 55). This form lists every exercise in the Review, Problem-Solving, and Quizzes sections of this book, providing a table so that you may record how many problems you've completed and what percentage you've answered correctly. After you've completed each section of exercises, be sure to fill out the respective portion of the progress report. It will document your progress and make it easier to recognize exactly what test sections or specific problem-types deserve most of your attention when taking the practice tests.

TAKING PRACTICE TESTS

In Step Four, there are four full-length ACT Science Reasoning Practice Tests. In these test sections, the problems not only mimic the real test in content and difficulty range, but they are also arranged in an order and with a frequency that simulates the real ACT.

Your instructor will ask you to complete some or all of these practice test problems in class, or he or she will assign them as homework. If you are taking these four test sections at home, you should take two with time restrictions and two without time restrictions. Taking the test without time restrictions will help you get a sense of how long it would take for you to comfortably and accurately solve a problem. Applying the time pressure then forces you to pace yourself as you would on the real test. If you complete all four of the practice test sections, any test anxiety you may have will be greatly reduced.

Be sure to record your efforts on the progress report form (p. 111). This form will be especially helpful after your course officially ends. At that point, you will make a plan for reviewing any areas in which you are still not performing as well as you would like.

MAKING SENSE OF YOUR OFFICIAL POST-TEST RESULTS

In order to know how far you've come since the pre-test, you have to take another official ACT, PLAN, or EXPLORE. Step Five serves this purpose. First, you will take the second official, retired test under actual testing conditions. Then, you will use the results to evaluate your progress and to determine exactly which problems would be the most beneficial for you to review.

The diagnostic post-test progress report (p. 173) is necessary to help you make a personal study plan, so be sure to record your Science Reasoning post-test results. In addition, Step Five contains a post-test bubble sheet. You can use this sheet to respond to all areas of the post-test, not just the Science Reasoning portion. *Use the other portions of this sheet only if your instructor tells you to do so.*

FIGURING OUT WHAT TO DO NEXT

The personal study plan progress report form (p. 185) will help you to create a prioritized list of what you still need to review before you take the actual ACT, PLAN, or EXPLORE. In addition, Step Six contains English, Mathematics, and Reading forms that are used as cross-curricular tools in order to reference your overall progress. Each form asks you to rank your ability to solve problems in each subject area of the review and strategies section and to specify the skills and strategies you need to focus on the most.

The three subject areas in this Science Reasoning book are:

- Data Representation Passages
- Research Summary Passages
- Conflicting Viewpoints Passages

Even after your Cambridge course has finished, you will find that this book is a great resource for continued science skills review and ACT, PLAN, or EXPLORE preparation.

STEP ONE: DIAGNOSTIC TESTING AND ASSESSMENT SERVICE

ACT • PLAN • EXPLORE SCIENCE REASONING

STEP ONE: DIAGNOSTIC TESTING AND ASSESSMENT SERVICE

AMERICA'S #1 STANDARDS-BASED SCHOOL IMPROVEMENT

Cambridge Course Concept Outline
STEP ONE

I. ACT • PLAN • EXPLORE DIAGNOSTIC PRE-TEST PROGRESS REPORTS (p. 13)

    A. ACT • PLAN EXPLORE DIAGNOSTIC PRE-TEST STUDENT PROGRESS REPORT (p. 13)

    B. ACT • PLAN EXPLORE DIAGNOSTIC PRE-TEST INSTRUCTOR PROGRESS REPORT (p. 15)

II. ACT • PLAN • EXPLORE PRE-TEST BUBBLE SHEET (p. 17)

PROGRESS REPORTS

ACT • PLAN • EXPLORE
DIAGNOSTIC PRE-TEST PROGRESS REPORT
(Student Copy)

DIRECTIONS: These progress reports are designed to help you make sense of your ACT, PLAN, or EXPLORE Science Reasoning Diagnostic Pre-Test results. Complete the diagnostic pre-test and record both the number and percentage of Science Reasoning problems that you answered correctly. Refer to your Cambridge Assessment Report when recording this information if your program has elected to use the Cambridge Assessment Service. Identify the date on which you completed the Science Reasoning section of the pre-test, and list the numbers of any problems that you would like your instructor to review in class.

Transfer this information to the Instructor Copy, and then give that report to your instructor.

Name _____ Student ID _____ Date _____

DIAGNOSTIC PRE-TEST
(Student Copy)

Test Section	Total # Possible	# Correct	% Correct	Date Completed	Problem #s to Review
ACT, PLAN, or EXPLORE SCIENCE REASONING					

Photocopying not allowed without Cambridge licensing agreement.

 **STEP ONE**

SCALE CONVERSION CHART
(Student Copy)

DIRECTIONS: This Scale Conversion Chart will help you translate the number of problems that you answered correctly into a scaled score. Record both the number and percentage of Science Reasoning problems that you answered correctly. Then, use the % Correct column to identify your raw score for this test. Find and record the raw score that corresponds to the scaled score that you earned on Table 1 in the back of your official, retired, test booklet.

Transfer this information to the Instructor Copy, and then give that report to your instructor.

DIAGNOSTIC PRE-TEST SCORE CALCULATION				
	Total # Possible	# Correct	% Correct	Scale Score
SCIENCE REASONING Diagnostic Pre-Test				

% CORRECT CHART							
Raw Score	40 Questions Total	60 Questions Total	75 Questions Total	Raw Score	40 Questions Total	60 Questions Total	75 Questions Total
1	3%	2%	1%	39	98%	65%	52%
2	5%	3%	3%	40	100%	67%	53%
3	8%	5%	4%	41		68%	55%
4	10%	7%	5%	42		70%	56%
5	13%	8%	7%	43		72%	57%
6	15%	10%	8%	44		73%	59%
7	18%	12%	9%	45		75%	60%
8	20%	13%	11%	46		77%	61%
9	23%	15%	13%	47		78%	63%
10	25%	17%	14%	48		80%	64%
11	28%	18%	15%	49		82%	65%
12	30%	20%	17%	50		83%	67%
13	33%	22%	18%	51		85%	68%
14	35%	23%	19%	52		87%	69%
15	38%	25%	20%	53		88%	71%
16	40%	27%	21%	54		90%	72%
17	43%	28%	23%	55		92%	73%
18	45%	30%	24%	56		93%	75%
19	48%	32%	25%	57		95%	76%
20	50%	33%	27%	58		97%	77%
21	53%	35%	28%	59		98%	79%
22	55%	37%	29%	60		100%	80%
23	58%	38%	31%	61			81%
24	60%	40%	32%	62			83%
25	63%	42%	33%	63			84%
26	65%	43%	35%	64			85%
27	68%	45%	36%	65			87%
28	70%	47%	37%	66			88%
29	73%	48%	39%	67			89%
30	75%	50%	40%	68			91%
31	78%	52%	41%	69			92%
32	80%	53%	43%	70			93%
33	83%	55%	44%	71			95%
34	85%	57%	45%	72			96%
35	88%	58%	47%	73			97%
36	90%	60%	48%	74			99%
37	93%	62%	49%	75			100%
38	95%	63%	51%				

PROGRESS REPORTS

ACT • PLAN • EXPLORE
DIAGNOSTIC PRE-TEST PROGRESS REPORT
(Instructor Copy)

DIRECTIONS: Transfer the information from your Student Copy to the Instructor Copy below. Leave the last two bolded columns blank. Your instructor will use them to evaluate your progress. When finished, give these reports to your instructor.

Student Name _____ Student ID _____ Date _____

DIAGNOSTIC PRE-TEST
(Instructor Copy)

Test Section	Total # Possible	# Correct	% Correct	Date Completed	Problem #s to Review	Instructor Skill Evaluation	
						Skills Review Needed? (Y or N)	*Skills Review Section and Problem Numbers Assigned*
ACT, PLAN, or EXPLORE SCIENCE REASONING							

Photocopying not allowed without Cambridge licensing agreement.

STEP ONE

SCALE CONVERSION CHART
(Instructor Copy)

DIRECTIONS: Transfer the information from your Student Copy to the Instructor Copy below. When finished, give these reports to your instructor.

DIAGNOSTIC PRE-TEST SCORE CALCULATION				
	Total # Possible	# Correct	% Correct	Scale Score
SCIENCE REASONING Diagnostic Pre-Test				

% CORRECT CHART							
Raw Score	40 Questions Total	60 Questions Total	75 Questions Total	Raw Score	40 Questions Total	60 Questions Total	75 Questions Total
1	3%	2%	1%	39	98%	65%	52%
2	5%	3%	3%	40	100%	67%	53%
3	8%	5%	4%	41		68%	55%
4	10%	7%	5%	42		70%	56%
5	13%	8%	7%	43		72%	57%
6	15%	10%	8%	44		73%	59%
7	18%	12%	9%	45		75%	60%
8	20%	13%	11%	46		77%	61%
9	23%	15%	13%	47		78%	63%
10	25%	17%	14%	48		80%	64%
11	28%	18%	15%	49		82%	65%
12	30%	20%	17%	50		83%	67%
13	33%	22%	18%	51		85%	68%
14	35%	23%	19%	52		87%	69%
15	38%	25%	20%	53		88%	71%
16	40%	27%	21%	54		90%	72%
17	43%	28%	23%	55		92%	73%
18	45%	30%	24%	56		93%	75%
19	48%	32%	25%	57		95%	76%
20	50%	33%	27%	58		97%	77%
21	53%	35%	28%	59		98%	79%
22	55%	37%	29%	60		100%	80%
23	58%	38%	31%	61			81%
24	60%	40%	32%	62			83%
25	63%	42%	33%	63			84%
26	65%	43%	35%	64			85%
27	68%	45%	36%	65			87%
28	70%	47%	37%	66			88%
29	73%	48%	39%	67			89%
30	75%	50%	40%	68			91%
31	78%	52%	41%	69			92%
32	80%	53%	43%	70			93%
33	83%	55%	44%	71			95%
34	85%	57%	45%	72			96%
35	88%	58%	47%	73			97%
36	90%	60%	48%	74			99%
37	93%	62%	49%	75			100%
38	95%	63%	51%				

ACT • PLAN • EXPLORE Pre-Test Bubble Sheet

Name ____________________ Student ID Number ____________________

Date ____________ Instructor ____________________ Course/Session Number ____________

TEST 1—ENGLISH

1 Ⓐ Ⓑ Ⓒ Ⓓ	16 Ⓕ Ⓖ Ⓗ Ⓙ	31 Ⓐ Ⓑ Ⓒ Ⓓ	46 Ⓕ Ⓖ Ⓗ Ⓙ	61 Ⓐ Ⓑ Ⓒ Ⓓ
2 Ⓕ Ⓖ Ⓗ Ⓙ	17 Ⓐ Ⓑ Ⓒ Ⓓ	32 Ⓕ Ⓖ Ⓗ Ⓙ	47 Ⓐ Ⓑ Ⓒ Ⓓ	62 Ⓕ Ⓖ Ⓗ Ⓙ
3 Ⓐ Ⓑ Ⓒ Ⓓ	18 Ⓕ Ⓖ Ⓗ Ⓙ	33 Ⓐ Ⓑ Ⓒ Ⓓ	48 Ⓕ Ⓖ Ⓗ Ⓙ	63 Ⓐ Ⓑ Ⓒ Ⓓ
4 Ⓕ Ⓖ Ⓗ Ⓙ	19 Ⓐ Ⓑ Ⓒ Ⓓ	34 Ⓕ Ⓖ Ⓗ Ⓙ	49 Ⓐ Ⓑ Ⓒ Ⓓ	64 Ⓕ Ⓖ Ⓗ Ⓙ
5 Ⓐ Ⓑ Ⓒ Ⓓ	20 Ⓕ Ⓖ Ⓗ Ⓙ	35 Ⓐ Ⓑ Ⓒ Ⓓ	50 Ⓕ Ⓖ Ⓗ Ⓙ	65 Ⓐ Ⓑ Ⓒ Ⓓ
6 Ⓕ Ⓖ Ⓗ Ⓙ	21 Ⓐ Ⓑ Ⓒ Ⓓ	36 Ⓕ Ⓖ Ⓗ Ⓙ	51 Ⓐ Ⓑ Ⓒ Ⓓ	66 Ⓕ Ⓖ Ⓗ Ⓙ
7 Ⓐ Ⓑ Ⓒ Ⓓ	22 Ⓕ Ⓖ Ⓗ Ⓙ	37 Ⓐ Ⓑ Ⓒ Ⓓ	52 Ⓕ Ⓖ Ⓗ Ⓙ	67 Ⓐ Ⓑ Ⓒ Ⓓ
8 Ⓕ Ⓖ Ⓗ Ⓙ	23 Ⓐ Ⓑ Ⓒ Ⓓ	38 Ⓕ Ⓖ Ⓗ Ⓙ	53 Ⓐ Ⓑ Ⓒ Ⓓ	68 Ⓕ Ⓖ Ⓗ Ⓙ
9 Ⓐ Ⓑ Ⓒ Ⓓ	24 Ⓕ Ⓖ Ⓗ Ⓙ	39 Ⓐ Ⓑ Ⓒ Ⓓ	54 Ⓕ Ⓖ Ⓗ Ⓙ	69 Ⓐ Ⓑ Ⓒ Ⓓ
10 Ⓕ Ⓖ Ⓗ Ⓙ	25 Ⓐ Ⓑ Ⓒ Ⓓ	40 Ⓕ Ⓖ Ⓗ Ⓙ	55 Ⓐ Ⓑ Ⓒ Ⓓ	70 Ⓕ Ⓖ Ⓗ Ⓙ
11 Ⓐ Ⓑ Ⓒ Ⓓ	26 Ⓕ Ⓖ Ⓗ Ⓙ	41 Ⓐ Ⓑ Ⓒ Ⓓ	56 Ⓕ Ⓖ Ⓗ Ⓙ	71 Ⓐ Ⓑ Ⓒ Ⓓ
12 Ⓕ Ⓖ Ⓗ Ⓙ	27 Ⓐ Ⓑ Ⓒ Ⓓ	42 Ⓕ Ⓖ Ⓗ Ⓙ	57 Ⓐ Ⓑ Ⓒ Ⓓ	72 Ⓕ Ⓖ Ⓗ Ⓙ
13 Ⓐ Ⓑ Ⓒ Ⓓ	28 Ⓕ Ⓖ Ⓗ Ⓙ	43 Ⓐ Ⓑ Ⓒ Ⓓ	58 Ⓕ Ⓖ Ⓗ Ⓙ	73 Ⓐ Ⓑ Ⓒ Ⓓ
14 Ⓕ Ⓖ Ⓗ Ⓙ	29 Ⓐ Ⓑ Ⓒ Ⓓ	44 Ⓕ Ⓖ Ⓗ Ⓙ	59 Ⓐ Ⓑ Ⓒ Ⓓ	74 Ⓕ Ⓖ Ⓗ Ⓙ
15 Ⓐ Ⓑ Ⓒ Ⓓ	30 Ⓕ Ⓖ Ⓗ Ⓙ	45 Ⓐ Ⓑ Ⓒ Ⓓ	60 Ⓕ Ⓖ Ⓗ Ⓙ	75 Ⓐ Ⓑ Ⓒ Ⓓ

TEST 2—MATHEMATICS

1 Ⓐ Ⓑ Ⓒ Ⓓ Ⓔ	13 Ⓐ Ⓑ Ⓒ Ⓓ Ⓔ	25 Ⓐ Ⓑ Ⓒ Ⓓ Ⓔ	37 Ⓐ Ⓑ Ⓒ Ⓓ Ⓔ	49 Ⓐ Ⓑ Ⓒ Ⓓ Ⓔ
2 Ⓕ Ⓖ Ⓗ Ⓙ Ⓚ	14 Ⓕ Ⓖ Ⓗ Ⓙ Ⓚ	26 Ⓕ Ⓖ Ⓗ Ⓙ Ⓚ	38 Ⓕ Ⓖ Ⓗ Ⓙ Ⓚ	50 Ⓕ Ⓖ Ⓗ Ⓙ Ⓚ
3 Ⓐ Ⓑ Ⓒ Ⓓ Ⓔ	15 Ⓐ Ⓑ Ⓒ Ⓓ Ⓔ	27 Ⓐ Ⓑ Ⓒ Ⓓ Ⓔ	39 Ⓐ Ⓑ Ⓒ Ⓓ Ⓔ	51 Ⓐ Ⓑ Ⓒ Ⓓ Ⓔ
4 Ⓕ Ⓖ Ⓗ Ⓙ Ⓚ	16 Ⓕ Ⓖ Ⓗ Ⓙ Ⓚ	28 Ⓕ Ⓖ Ⓗ Ⓙ Ⓚ	40 Ⓕ Ⓖ Ⓗ Ⓙ Ⓚ	52 Ⓕ Ⓖ Ⓗ Ⓙ Ⓚ
5 Ⓐ Ⓑ Ⓒ Ⓓ Ⓔ	17 Ⓐ Ⓑ Ⓒ Ⓓ Ⓔ	29 Ⓐ Ⓑ Ⓒ Ⓓ Ⓔ	41 Ⓐ Ⓑ Ⓒ Ⓓ Ⓔ	53 Ⓐ Ⓑ Ⓒ Ⓓ Ⓔ
6 Ⓕ Ⓖ Ⓗ Ⓙ Ⓚ	18 Ⓕ Ⓖ Ⓗ Ⓙ Ⓚ	30 Ⓕ Ⓖ Ⓗ Ⓙ Ⓚ	42 Ⓕ Ⓖ Ⓗ Ⓙ Ⓚ	54 Ⓕ Ⓖ Ⓗ Ⓙ Ⓚ
7 Ⓐ Ⓑ Ⓒ Ⓓ Ⓔ	19 Ⓐ Ⓑ Ⓒ Ⓓ Ⓔ	31 Ⓐ Ⓑ Ⓒ Ⓓ Ⓔ	43 Ⓐ Ⓑ Ⓒ Ⓓ Ⓔ	55 Ⓐ Ⓑ Ⓒ Ⓓ Ⓔ
8 Ⓕ Ⓖ Ⓗ Ⓙ Ⓚ	20 Ⓕ Ⓖ Ⓗ Ⓙ Ⓚ	32 Ⓕ Ⓖ Ⓗ Ⓙ Ⓚ	44 Ⓕ Ⓖ Ⓗ Ⓙ Ⓚ	56 Ⓕ Ⓖ Ⓗ Ⓙ Ⓚ
9 Ⓐ Ⓑ Ⓒ Ⓓ Ⓔ	21 Ⓐ Ⓑ Ⓒ Ⓓ Ⓔ	33 Ⓐ Ⓑ Ⓒ Ⓓ Ⓔ	45 Ⓐ Ⓑ Ⓒ Ⓓ Ⓔ	57 Ⓐ Ⓑ Ⓒ Ⓓ Ⓔ
10 Ⓕ Ⓖ Ⓗ Ⓙ Ⓚ	22 Ⓕ Ⓖ Ⓗ Ⓙ Ⓚ	34 Ⓕ Ⓖ Ⓗ Ⓙ Ⓚ	46 Ⓕ Ⓖ Ⓗ Ⓙ Ⓚ	58 Ⓕ Ⓖ Ⓗ Ⓙ Ⓚ
11 Ⓐ Ⓑ Ⓒ Ⓓ Ⓔ	23 Ⓐ Ⓑ Ⓒ Ⓓ Ⓔ	35 Ⓐ Ⓑ Ⓒ Ⓓ Ⓔ	47 Ⓐ Ⓑ Ⓒ Ⓓ Ⓔ	59 Ⓐ Ⓑ Ⓒ Ⓓ Ⓔ
12 Ⓕ Ⓖ Ⓗ Ⓙ Ⓚ	24 Ⓕ Ⓖ Ⓗ Ⓙ Ⓚ	36 Ⓕ Ⓖ Ⓗ Ⓙ Ⓚ	48 Ⓕ Ⓖ Ⓗ Ⓙ Ⓚ	60 Ⓕ Ⓖ Ⓗ Ⓙ Ⓚ

TEST 3—READING

1 Ⓐ Ⓑ Ⓒ Ⓓ	9 Ⓐ Ⓑ Ⓒ Ⓓ	17 Ⓐ Ⓑ Ⓒ Ⓓ	25 Ⓐ Ⓑ Ⓒ Ⓓ	33 Ⓐ Ⓑ Ⓒ Ⓓ
2 Ⓕ Ⓖ Ⓗ Ⓙ	10 Ⓕ Ⓖ Ⓗ Ⓙ	18 Ⓕ Ⓖ Ⓗ Ⓙ	26 Ⓕ Ⓖ Ⓗ Ⓙ	34 Ⓕ Ⓖ Ⓗ Ⓙ
3 Ⓐ Ⓑ Ⓒ Ⓓ	11 Ⓐ Ⓑ Ⓒ Ⓓ	19 Ⓐ Ⓑ Ⓒ Ⓓ	27 Ⓐ Ⓑ Ⓒ Ⓓ	35 Ⓐ Ⓑ Ⓒ Ⓓ
4 Ⓕ Ⓖ Ⓗ Ⓙ	12 Ⓕ Ⓖ Ⓗ Ⓙ	20 Ⓕ Ⓖ Ⓗ Ⓙ	28 Ⓕ Ⓖ Ⓗ Ⓙ	36 Ⓕ Ⓖ Ⓗ Ⓙ
5 Ⓐ Ⓑ Ⓒ Ⓓ	13 Ⓐ Ⓑ Ⓒ Ⓓ	21 Ⓐ Ⓑ Ⓒ Ⓓ	29 Ⓐ Ⓑ Ⓒ Ⓓ	37 Ⓐ Ⓑ Ⓒ Ⓓ
6 Ⓕ Ⓖ Ⓗ Ⓙ	14 Ⓕ Ⓖ Ⓗ Ⓙ	22 Ⓕ Ⓖ Ⓗ Ⓙ	30 Ⓕ Ⓖ Ⓗ Ⓙ	38 Ⓕ Ⓖ Ⓗ Ⓙ
7 Ⓐ Ⓑ Ⓒ Ⓓ	15 Ⓐ Ⓑ Ⓒ Ⓓ	23 Ⓐ Ⓑ Ⓒ Ⓓ	31 Ⓐ Ⓑ Ⓒ Ⓓ	39 Ⓐ Ⓑ Ⓒ Ⓓ
8 Ⓕ Ⓖ Ⓗ Ⓙ	16 Ⓕ Ⓖ Ⓗ Ⓙ	24 Ⓕ Ⓖ Ⓗ Ⓙ	32 Ⓕ Ⓖ Ⓗ Ⓙ	40 Ⓕ Ⓖ Ⓗ Ⓙ

TEST 4—SCIENCE REASONING

1 Ⓐ Ⓑ Ⓒ Ⓓ	9 Ⓐ Ⓑ Ⓒ Ⓓ	17 Ⓐ Ⓑ Ⓒ Ⓓ	25 Ⓐ Ⓑ Ⓒ Ⓓ	33 Ⓐ Ⓑ Ⓒ Ⓓ
2 Ⓕ Ⓖ Ⓗ Ⓙ	10 Ⓕ Ⓖ Ⓗ Ⓙ	18 Ⓕ Ⓖ Ⓗ Ⓙ	26 Ⓕ Ⓖ Ⓗ Ⓙ	34 Ⓕ Ⓖ Ⓗ Ⓙ
3 Ⓐ Ⓑ Ⓒ Ⓓ	11 Ⓐ Ⓑ Ⓒ Ⓓ	19 Ⓐ Ⓑ Ⓒ Ⓓ	27 Ⓐ Ⓑ Ⓒ Ⓓ	35 Ⓐ Ⓑ Ⓒ Ⓓ
4 Ⓕ Ⓖ Ⓗ Ⓙ	12 Ⓕ Ⓖ Ⓗ Ⓙ	20 Ⓕ Ⓖ Ⓗ Ⓙ	28 Ⓕ Ⓖ Ⓗ Ⓙ	36 Ⓕ Ⓖ Ⓗ Ⓙ
5 Ⓐ Ⓑ Ⓒ Ⓓ	13 Ⓐ Ⓑ Ⓒ Ⓓ	21 Ⓐ Ⓑ Ⓒ Ⓓ	29 Ⓐ Ⓑ Ⓒ Ⓓ	37 Ⓐ Ⓑ Ⓒ Ⓓ
6 Ⓕ Ⓖ Ⓗ Ⓙ	14 Ⓕ Ⓖ Ⓗ Ⓙ	22 Ⓕ Ⓖ Ⓗ Ⓙ	30 Ⓕ Ⓖ Ⓗ Ⓙ	38 Ⓕ Ⓖ Ⓗ Ⓙ
7 Ⓐ Ⓑ Ⓒ Ⓓ	15 Ⓐ Ⓑ Ⓒ Ⓓ	23 Ⓐ Ⓑ Ⓒ Ⓓ	31 Ⓐ Ⓑ Ⓒ Ⓓ	39 Ⓐ Ⓑ Ⓒ Ⓓ
8 Ⓕ Ⓖ Ⓗ Ⓙ	16 Ⓕ Ⓖ Ⓗ Ⓙ	24 Ⓕ Ⓖ Ⓗ Ⓙ	32 Ⓕ Ⓖ Ⓗ Ⓙ	40 Ⓕ Ⓖ Ⓗ Ⓙ

STEP TWO: SKILLS REVIEW

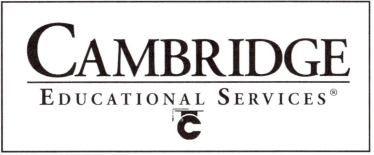

ACT • PLAN • EXPLORE SCIENCE REASONING

STEP TWO: SKILLS REVIEW

AMERICA'S #1 STANDARDS-BASED SCHOOL IMPROVEMENT

Cambridge Course Concept Outline
STEP TWO

I. **ACT • PLAN • EXPLORE SCIENCE REASONING STEP TWO PROGRESS REPORTS** (p. 25)

    A. **ACT • PLAN EXPLORE SCIENCE REASONING STEP TWO STUDENT PROGRESS REPORT** (p. 25)

    B. **ACT • PLAN EXPLORE SCIENCE REASONING STEP TWO INSTRUCTOR PROGRESS REPORT** (p. 27)

II. **SCIENCE SKILLS REVIEW** (p. 31)

    A. **UNDERSTANDING SCIENTIFIC INFORMATION** (p. 31)

    B. **BASICS OF EXPERIMENTAL DESIGN** (p. 33)
        1. EXERCISE 1—BASICS OF EXPERIMENTAL DESIGN (p. 35)

    C. **DATA ORGANIZATION IN CONTROLLED EXPERIMENTS** (p. 36)
        1. EXERCISE 2—DATA ORGANIZATION IN CONTROLLED EXPERIMENTS (p. 40)

    D. **PRESENTATION OF CONFLICTING VIEWPOINTS** (p. 42)
        1. EXERCISE 3—PRESENTATION OF CONFLICTING VIEWPOINTS (p. 43)

    E. **EXERCISE FOUR—SCIENCE REASONING PASSAGES** (p. 44)

PROGRESS REPORTS

ACT • PLAN • EXPLORE SCIENCE REASONING
STEP TWO PROGRESS REPORT
(Student Copy)

DIRECTIONS: These progress reports are designed to help you monitor your Science Skills Review progress. Complete the assigned problems corresponding to each Science Skills Review lesson, correct your answers, and record both the number and percentage of problems that you answered correctly. Identify the date on which you completed each exercise. List the numbers of any problems that you would like your instructor to review in class.

Transfer this information to the Instructor Copy, and then give that report to your instructor.

Name _____ Student ID _____ Date _____

SCIENCE SKILLS REVIEW
(Student Copy)

Exercise	Total # Possible	Assigned	# Correct	% Correct	Date Completed	Problem #s to Review
1. Basics of Experimental Design (p. 35)	7					
2. Data Organization in Controlled Experiments (p. 40)	9					
3. Presentation of Conflicting Viewpoints (p. 43)	4					
4. Science Reasoning Passages (p. 44)	24					

Photocopying not allowed without Cambridge licensing agreement.

PROGRESS REPORTS

ACT • PLAN • EXPLORE SCIENCE REASONING
STEP TWO PROGRESS REPORT
(Instructor Copy)

DIRECTIONS: Transfer the information from your Student Copy to the Instructor Copy below. Leave the last three bolded columns blank. Your instructor will use them to evaluate your progress. When finished, give these reports to your instructor.

Student Name _____ Student ID _____ Date _____

SCIENCE SKILLS REVIEW
(Instructor Copy)

Exercise	Total # Possible	Total # Assigned	# Correct	% Correct	Date Completed	Problem #s to Review	**Mastered**	**Partially Mastered**	**Not Mastered**
1. Basics of Experimental Design (p. 35)	7								
2. Data Organization in Controlled Experiments (p. 40)	9								
3. Presentation of Conflicting Viewpoints (p. 43)	4								
4. Science Reasoning Passages (p. 44)	24								

Photocopying not allowed without Cambridge licensing agreement.

ACT • PLAN • EXPLORE SCIENCE REASONING

SCIENCE SKILLS REVIEW

Understanding Scientific Information

The purpose of the ACT Science Reasoning Test is to examine your ability to read and understand scientific information. Rather than testing your knowledge of science facts, the questions will measure your reasoning and problem-solving skills related to science. The test emphasizes the ability to reason using the skills of a scientist, not the recall of scientific content or specific mathematical skills used in science.

Studying and completing the activities in this review supplement will enhance your science reasoning skills. This supplement will examine how an experiment is set up, provide guidelines for organizing data collected by observation and experimentation, and present a list of terms that are often found in the passages and questions.

Science Reasoning Passages

The scientific skills measured on the ACT Science Reasoning Test are tested by questions that ask about scientific information in three different types of reading passages: research summaries, data representation, and conflicting viewpoints. The scientific information in these types of passages has been gathered by observation and experimentation.

1. Research Summary Passages

The ***research summary*** passages consist of descriptions of how specific experiments were carried out and a summary of the experimental results. In the research summary passages, you may be required to identify the differences in design of the experiments, predict the outcome based on results of an experiment, or predict the outcome of an experiment if the design is changed. You may also be required to identify a hypothesis that is being investigated, select a hypothesis supported by the results of an experiment, determine the conclusion supported by the given results of an experiment, or select an experiment that could be conducted in order to test another hypothesis.

2. Data Representation Passages

The ***data representation*** passages present scientific information in the form of graphs, tables, and figures. In data representation passages, you may be asked to select a conclusion that can be supported by the data, determine the relationship between two variables, or select an explanation for a given experimental result. You may also be required to determine if a conclusion is consistent with the information given, apply the given data to a new situation, or determine what the slope of a line on a graph represents.

3. Conflicting Viewpoints Passages

The ***conflicting viewpoints*** passages present differing hypotheses, theories, or viewpoints of two or three scientists. In the conflicting viewpoints passages, you may be required to determine each scientist's position, select the evidence that supports the viewpoints of both scientists, or determine the similarities and differences of the viewpoints of the scientists. You may also be asked to determine the strengths and weaknesses of the viewpoints, figure out how new information would affect either viewpoint, or predict evidence that would support a scientist's viewpoint.

Presentation of Additional Information

While more commonly found in data representation passages, any Science Reasoning passage may include information organized in the form of charts, diagrams, figures, graphs, illustrations, and tables like those found in science journals and textbooks. Typically, on the test, you will be asked to read, interpret, and analyze data presented in these forms.

STEP TWO

Science Reasoning Vocabulary

The following list is composed of terms that are commonly found in the passages and questions. Understanding the definitions and uses of these terms will help you better understand the passage or question in which they are used.

absolute: existing independent of any other cause
accuracy: freedom from mistake; exactness; the relationship between the gradation on a measuring device and the actual standard for the quantity being measured
adverse: acting against or in an opposite direction
analogous: similar or comparable in certain respects
analyze: to study the relationship of the parts of something by analysis
application: ability to put to a practical use; having something to do with the matter at hand
approximately: nearly; an estimate or figure that is almost exact
argument: a reason for or against something
assumption: something accepted as true
comprehend: to understand fully
concentration: the ratio of the amount of solute to the amount of solvent or solution
conclusion: a final decision based on facts, experience, or reasoning
confirm: to make sure of the truth of something
consequence: something produced by a cause or condition
consistent: in agreement; firm; changeless
constant: remaining steady and unchanged
contradiction: a statement in opposition to another
control group: experimental group in which conditions are controlled
controlled experiment: one in which the condition suspected to cause an effect is compared to one without the suspected condition
controlled variable: a factor in an experiment that remains constant
correlation: a close connection between two ideas or sets of data
criticism: a finding of fault; disapproval
definitive: most nearly complete or accurate
demonstrate: to explain by use of examples or experiments
dependence: a state of being controlled by something else
dependent variable: result or change that occurs due to the part of an experiment being tested (positioned on the vertical *y*-axis)
diminish: to make smaller or less; decrease in size
direct relationship: the connection between two variables that show the same effect (*i.e.*, both increase or both decrease)
effective: producing or able to produce a desired condition
estimation: forming a calculation based on incomplete data
ethical: following accepted rules of behavior
evaluation: the result of a finding; estimating the value of something
evidence: that which serves to prove or disprove something
examine: to look at or check carefully
expectation: the extent of a chance that something will occur
experiment: a test made to find something out
experimental design: the plan for a controlled experiment
experimental group: the experimental part in which all conditions are kept the same except for the condition being tested
explanation: a statement that makes something clear
extrapolation: estimating a value for one characteristic that is beyond the range of a given value of another characteristic
figure: a picture that explains
fundamental: a basic part
generalization: something given as a broad statement or conclusion
hypothesis: testable explanation of a question or problem
illustrate: to make clear by using examples
imply: to suggest rather than to say plainly
inconsistent: not in agreement
incorporate: to join or unite closely into a single body

independent variable: in a controlled experiment, the variable that is being changed (positioned on the horizontal *x*-axis)
indication: the act of pointing out or pointing to something
indicator: any device that measures, records, or visibly points out; any of various substances used to point out, such as, a cause, treatment, or outcome on an action
ingredient: any of the components of which something is made
interpolation: estimating a value that falls between two known values; a "best-fit line" on a graph
interpretation: the act of telling the meaning of; explanation
inverse (indirect) relationship: the connection between two variables that shows the opposite effect (*i.e.*, when the value of one variable increases, the value of the other variable deceases)
investigate: to study by close and careful observation
irregular: not continuous or coming at set times
issue: something that is questioned
judgment: an opinion formed by examining and comparing
justify: to prove or show to be right or reasonable
legend: a title, description, or key accompanying a figure or map
maximum: as great as possible in amount or degree
measurement: the act of finding out the size or amount of something
mechanism: the parts or steps that make up a process or activity
minimum: as small as possible in amount or degree
model: a pattern or figure of something to be made
modify: to make changes in something
observation: the act of noting and recording facts and events
opinion: a belief based on experience and on seeing certain facts
optimum: the best or most favorable degree, condition, or amount
pattern: a model, guide, or plan used in making things; definite direction, tendency, or characteristics
perform: to carry out; accomplish
phenomenon: an observable fact or event
precision: the quality of being exactly stated; exact arrangement
predict: to figure out and tell beforehand
preference: a choosing of or liking for one thing rather than another
probability: the quality of being reasonably sure but not certain of something happening or being true
procedure: the way in which an action or actions is carried out
proponent: one who supports a cause
proportional: any quantities or measurements having the same fixed relationship in degree or number
reasonable: showing or containing sound thought
refute: to prove wrong by argument or evidence
relationship: the state of being connected
replicate: to copy or reproduce
revise: to look over again; to correct or improve
simulation: the act or process of simulating a system or process
study: a careful examination and investigation of an event
suggest: to offer as an idea
summarize: to state briefly
support: to provide evidence
theory: a general rule offered to explain experiences or facts
translate: to change from one state or form to another
treatment: to expose to some action
underlying: to form the support for something
unit: a fixed quantity used as a standard of measurement
validity: based on evidence that can be supported
value: the quantity or amount for which a symbol stands
variable: that which can be changed
viewpoint: opinion; judgment

Science Skills Review

Basics of Experimental Design

The Science Reasoning passages describe scientific methods that may be unfamiliar to you, but are commonly used by scientists to interpret and analyze scientific information. You need to be familiar with these basics of experimental design in order to understand the complete meaning of the passages and questions.

Types of Research

Scientists regularly attempt to identify and solve problems by investigating the world around them. Different scientists may use different approaches to conduct their investigations. *Qualitative*, or descriptive, research is based generally on observable data only.

EXAMPLE:
A field biologist may observe coral reefs in order to determine if the loss of this habitat would threaten the extinction of many species that live in the coral reefs.

Quantitative research is based on the collection of numerical data—usually by counting or measuring.

EXAMPLE:
A laboratory biologist may investigate the factors that affect the flow of substances across cell membranes. Numerical data is collected by measuring the change in mass of a cellophane bag that is filled with a sugar solution and then placed in a beaker of pure water.

Forming and Testing Hypotheses

Scientists normally *form a hypothesis* and then test it through observation, experimentation, and/or prediction. A hypothesis is defined as a possible explanation of a question or problem that can be formally tested. A hypothesis can be thought of as a prediction about why something occurs or about the relationship between two or more variables.

Scientists describe an experiment as a procedure that *tests a hypothesis* by the process of collecting information under controlled conditions. Based on the experimental results, scientists can determine whether or not the hypothesis is correct or must be modified and re-tested. Testing hypotheses through experiments is at the core of scientific investigations or studies.

An important part of testing a hypothesis is identifying the *variables* that are part of an experiment. A variable is any condition that can change in an experiment. The goal of a controlled experiment is to keep all of the variables constant, except the one under study, which is called the *independent variable*. The experimenter determines the independent variable, and it can change independently of other variables. The independent variable is the only variable that can affect the outcome of an experiment by causing a change that can be observed or measured. The changed conditions are called the *dependent variables* because they are the result of, or dependent upon, the changes in the independent variable.

Scientists attempt to test only one independent variable at a time so that he or she knows which condition produced the effect. *Controlled variables*, or controls, are conditions that could affect the outcome of an experiment but do not, because they are held constant. Controls are used to eliminate the possibility that conditions other than those that are a part of an experiment may affect the outcome of the experiment.

The statement of a testable hypothesis must be structured so that it will demonstrate how a change in the independent variable can cause an observed or measured change in the dependent variable. A hypothesis may be typically structured as follows: the independent variable will describe how it is changed; the dependent variable will describe the effect.

EXAMPLE:
In a controlled experiment, in order to determine the effect of a high protein diet on the growth rate of rats, the independent variable would be the exposure to a high protein diet, while the dependent variable would be the effect on the growth rate. A possible hypothesis for this experiment may be stated as follows: When the amount of protein is increased in the diet of rats, then their growth rate will increase.

Design of Controlled Experiments

The design of controlled experiments involves two groups: the ***control group*** and the ***experimental group***. In the control group, all variables are kept the same. In the experimental group, all conditions are kept the same as the control group except the condition that is being tested. The variable being tested in the experimental group is the independent variable.

The control group and the experimental group must be as similar as possible at the beginning of a controlled experiment. The only difference in the design of the two groups is the addition of the independent variable that is tested in the experimental group. It is common in a controlled experiment to have more than one experimental group to represent the possible variations in the conditions of the independent variable. All other variables that could affect the outcome of the experiment are held constant.

EXAMPLE:

In the previous experiment about the effect of a high protein diet on the growth rate of rats, a large test population of commonly similar rats would be randomly, yet equally (in size), divided into two smaller groups—the control group and the experimental group.

The rats in the above experiment are randomly divided to ensure that both groups are representative samples of the original population. If the test group is not representative of the original population, other uncontrolled conditions could affect the outcome of the experiment. If there are any uncontrolled conditions in either group, it could be argued that any experimental results would be due to differences in the composition of the different test groups instead of a result of the independent variable.

Continuing the development of the experiment, we see that the establishment of certain conditions makes this a controlled experiment.

EXAMPLE:

The rats in the control group are exposed to the same conditions as the rats in the experimental group, except for the amount of protein in their diet. The control group rats are given a diet with the normal amount of protein. The rats in the experimental group are exposed to a high protein diet (independent variable), in addition to the same conditions as the control group. (It would be possible to have more than one experimental group with each having a greater amount of protein.) The other conditions that could change, such as the temperature, amount of food and water, and amount of living space, are held constant for both groups of rats.

These conditions are the controls necessary for this experiment to be considered a controlled experiment. The data collected can be used to determine if the hypothesis is correct, and it will ultimately lead to the forming of a conclusion. The figure below illustrates the design of this experiment.

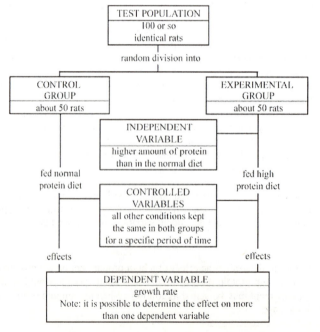

SCIENCE SKILLS REVIEW

EXERCISE 1

Basics of Experimental Design

DIRECTIONS: Read the description of the following controlled experiment and answer the accompanying questions. Answers are on page 205.

An experiment was carried out to determine the effect of temperature on the heart rate of frogs. In the experiment, 100 frogs were removed from a large enclosure and separated randomly into four equal groups: A, B, C, and D. Each group was maintained in a separate container at a different constant temperature: Group A at 5° C; Group B at 15° C; Group C at 25° C; and Group D at 35° C. All other conditions, such as the size, type, age, and number of the frogs, as well as the size of the container and the amount of light, were the same for all groups of frogs.

1. The purpose of the experiment is to: _____

2. The independent variable is: _____

3. The dependent variable is: _____

4. Write a possible hypothesis by filling in the blanks in the following sentence.

    When the _____ is _____,
        (independent variable) (describe how it is changed)

    then the _____ will _____.
        (dependent variable) (describe the effect)

5. The controlled variables are: _____

6. The control group(s) is (are): _____

7. The experimental group(s) is (are): _____

 STEP TWO

Data Organization in Controlled Experiments

After collecting data, a scientist must determine the most appropriate way to present the information so that it can be easily interpreted and analyzed. The two most common ways that scientists report their data are tables and graphs. These pictorial representations are easy ways to show where a pattern, trend, or relationship exists. The tables and graphs can be organized in a variety of ways, but there are some generally accepted basic guidelines.

Tables

Generally, *tables* are a series of vertical columns, subdivided horizontally into rows. The number of columns and rows depends on the kind and amount of data collected. In the most basic tables, there is a column for both the independent variable and the dependent variable. In complex tables, the columns may be subdivided to represent additional variations in the conditions of the independent and dependent variables. The rows include the data for the repeated collection of data. When recording data in a table, the values of the independent variable are arranged in an ordered manner—numerical data are arranged from the largest to the smallest or from the smallest to the largest. When relevant, units of measurement for the variables are included. A heading or title communicates the purpose of the experiment.

Relationships between variables may be direct, indirect (inverse), or constant. A ***direct relationship*** occurs when one variable increases and the other increases, or when one variable decreases and the other decreases. An ***indirect***, or inverse, ***relationship*** occurs when one variable increases and the other decreases. A ***constant relationship*** occurs when a change in one variable has no effect on the other variable.

EXAMPLE:

The table below makes it easy to see that there is a direct relationship between the temperature and the heart rate of frogs.

	The Effect of Temperature on Frog Heart Rates	
Group	*Temperature (°C)* (independent variable)	*Average Heart Rate (per minute)* (dependent variable)
A	5	10
B	15	20
C	25	30
D	35	40

As the temperature increases, so does the heart rate of the frog. If the heart rate had decreased when the temperature increased, then there would have been an indirect relationship between the two variables. If the heart rate had remained the same when the temperature was increased or decreased, then the relationship would have been considered constant.

Graphs

Scientists often collect large amounts of data while doing experiments. It may not be possible to clearly present the data in the form of a table. The arrangement of the data in a table may not easily or adequately show a pattern, trend, or relationship. Usually, a well-constructed *graph* can communicate experiment results more clearly than a data table. Generally, when the values of the variables are arranged in a graph, the patterns, trends, and relationships are more apparent than when those same values are arranged in a table. Three of the most useful kinds of graphs are line, bar, and circle (pie) graphs.

1. Line Graphs

A *line graph* has four basic parts: ***horizontal axis*** (*A*), ***vertical axis*** (*B*), ***line*** (*C*), and ***heading*** (*D*) or title. A line graph is used to show the relationship between two variables. The variables being compared are positioned on the two axes of the graph.

SCIENCE SKILLS REVIEW

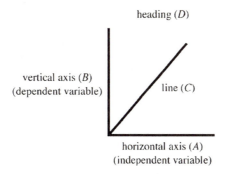

The ***independent variable*** is always positioned on the horizontal axis, called the ***x-axis***. The experimenter can change the value of the independent variable and those values are marked off along the horizontal axis.

The ***dependent variable*** is always positioned on the vertical axis, the ***y-axis***. The dependent variable, such as the rate of a chemical reaction, is any change that results from changing the value of the independent variable. Values of the dependent variable are marked off along the vertical axis.

The data that describe the relationship between the variables appear on the graph as dots, connected to form a line or curve. Each dot, or plot, represents the relationship that exists between a measurement on the vertical axis and a measurement on the horizontal axis. The slope of the line that is created by the connected points represents the relationship between the two variables. If more than one line appears on the same graph, each line represents variations in the conditions of the independent variable. Additionally, the lines may be curved rather than straight. However, typically, this does not affect the general relationship illustrated.

Finally, as with a table, the heading or title communicates the purpose of the experiment.

EXAMPLE:

The slopes of the lines in the following three graphs illustrate the typical kinds of relationships between variables shown in a line graph.

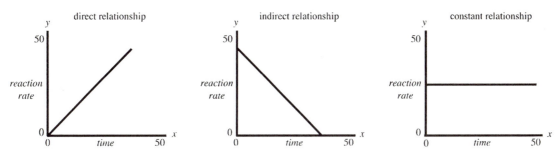

The first graph illustrates a direct relationship—as time increases, the reaction rate increases. The second graph illustrates an indirect relationship—as time increases, the reaction rate decreases. The third graph illustrates a constant relationship—as time increases, the rate of reaction remains the same; that is, time had no effect on the rate of reaction.

EXAMPLE:

The following graphs illustrate variations on those graphs from the previous example.

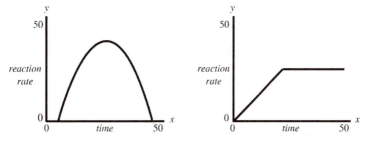

The first graph indicates that as time increases, the reaction rate increases to an ***optimum***, or best, rate, and then decreases. The second graph indicates that as time increases, the reaction rate increases, and then becomes constant.

STEP TWO

Since the collection of experimental data is often subject to error, data points plotted on a line may not be directly connected. The graph may show only scattered points so that a smooth line may not be constructed. As a result, another type of line graph is required to illustrate an estimate of a value that falls between two known values on the line. A "***best-fit***" line, a line that comes close to all of the points, must be constructed. This process is called ***interpolation***.

EXAMPLE:

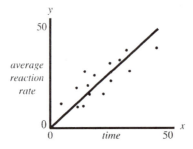

The scattered points in the graph above illustrate data collected from several reactions over an increasing period of time. To determine the relationship between average reaction rate and time, a line is drawn so that an approximately equal number of points fall on either side of the line. This graph indicates a direct relationship between the reaction rate and time.

Sometimes, it is necessary for a scientist to estimate a value for one variable based on a given value of another variable that is beyond the limits of the available data shown on the graph. The scientist must then extend the line on the graph based on the data given. The process is called ***extrapolation***.

EXAMPLE:

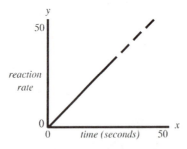

If the line is relatively straight, as shown in the graph above, the line can be extended far enough so that the values called for can be included. Suppose the scientist wanted to determine the reaction rate at a time of 50 seconds. By extending the line to follow the apparent pattern, it is possible to predict the reaction rate.

When using the technique of extrapolation, a scientist must be careful not to make a possible false assumption that the relationship will continue unchanged indefinitely. It is possible that beyond a certain time, an unexpected change in the independent variable will result in an unpredicted change in the dependent variable. When the graph line is a curve, it is necessary to use one's best judgment to extend the line to follow the apparent pattern.

EXAMPLE:

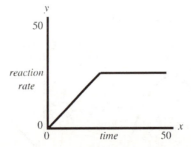

In the graph above, if the data collection had stopped after about 15 units of time, the scientist may have inaccurately predicted that the reaction rate could continue to increase.

2. Bar Graphs

A ***bar graph*** is similar to a line graph, but it is better for making simple comparisons. This type of graph is typically used to display data that does not continuously change. Bar graphs present related data side by side so the data can be easily compared.

The basic setup of a bar graph is similar to a line graph in that there is a horizontal x-axis and a vertical y-axis. The independent variable is positioned on the x-axis and the dependent variable is on the y-axis. Thick bars rather than data points show relationships among data. The bars representing the values of the independent variable, on the x-axis, are drawn up to an imaginary point where they would intersect with the values of the dependent variable on the y-axis if these values were extended. Generally, the taller the bar, the greater the value it represents.

Note that bar graphs may be configured horizontally, as well as vertically. In a horizontal configuration, the longer the bar, the greater the value it represents. Generally, a heading describes the presented data.

EXAMPLE:

The following bar graph shows the percentage of the human population having each blood type.

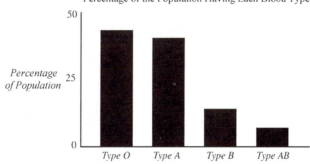

The independent variable is the different blood types found in the population. The dependent variable is the percentage of each blood type. The graph shows that the most common blood type is Type O, while the least common is Type AB.

3. Circle Graphs

Circle graphs use a circle divided into sections to display data. A circle graph is sometimes called a pie chart because it looks like a pie cut up into pieces. Each section of the graph represents one of the categories of a particular subject. The whole circle represents 100%, or all of the parts, of the data for all of the categories. The bigger the section, the larger the value it represents. Circle graphs are typically used to illustrate information that is collected by observation rather than by experimentation.

EXAMPLE:

The following circle graph represents the amount of organisms in a sample of soil.

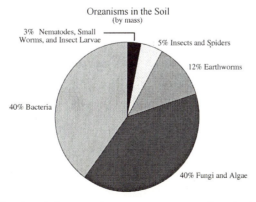

As indicated in the graph, bacteria, fungi, and algae, are the most common organisms in the soil. Each group makes up 40% of the total amount of organisms.

STEP TWO

EXERCISE 2

Data Organization in Controlled Experiments

DIRECTIONS: Read the descriptions of the following controlled experiments and answer the accompanying questions. Answers are on page 205.

EXPERIMENT I

A laboratory investigation was performed to determine the length of time necessary to digest starch (carbohydrates). Ten grams of potato were added to 15 milliliters of an enzyme solution and placed in a test tube. The percentage of starch digested was recorded over a 24-hour period, as can be seen in the table below. A line graph is also provided to illustrate the relationship between the variables.

Carbohydrate Digestion over a 24-Hour Period	
Time (hours)	Percentage of Carbohydrates Digested
0	0
4	5
8	15
12	50
16	75
20	85
24	90

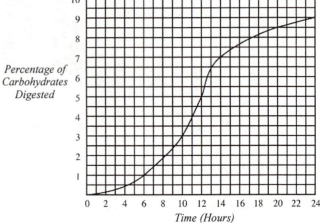

Carbohydrate Digestion over a 24-Hour Period

1. The independent variable is: _____.

2. The dependent variable is: _____.

3. The independent variable is on the _____ axis.

4. The dependent variable is on the _____ axis.

5. The slope of the line indicates that generally as the amount of time (increases, decreases, stays constant), the percentage of carbohydrates digested (increases, decreases, stays constant).

6. According to the data, during which four-hour period did the greatest amount of carbohydrate digestion occur?

   A. 0-4 hours
   B. 4-8 hours
   C. 8-12 hours
   D. 20-24 hours

EXPERIMENT II

The following graph illustrates the results of an investigation comparing the salt content in the urine of two mammals (humans and kangaroo rats) with the salt content of seawater.

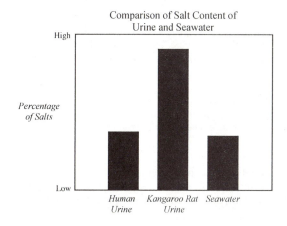

7. The independent variable is: _____.

8. The dependent variable is: _____.

9. The mammal with a percentage of salt in its urine closest to the percentage of salt in seawater is:

   _____.

 STEP TWO

Presentation of Conflicting Viewpoints

In experiments performed in the laboratory, a scientist studies a characteristic of matter or energy and attempts to find factors that will affect this characteristic. In typical experiments, scientists get to manipulate or change the independent variable. The independent variable, sometimes called the "causal variable," is assumed to cause any resulting change in the dependent variable.

Many problems (dependent variables) studied by scientists cannot be studied in the lab. An example might be the cause of cancer in humans. Scientists cannot put humans in a lab and treat them with substances that cause cancer. Instead, they must look at groups of individuals who get cancer and groups that do not get cancer, and determine the "secret" independent variable that caused the problem from the collected data. "Cause" is a strong word in science and it generally leads to arguments among scientists. Differences in opinions lead us to *conflicting viewpoints* on the ACT.

Science Reasoning "Conflicting Viewpoints" passages can always be recognized because they are labeled with names such as Scientist I and Scientist II. The scientists may be labeled with more specificity, for example, a chemistry passage may have Chemist I arguing with Chemist II about a chemistry problem; however, the argument is over the independent variable.

EXAMPLE:

Ask yourself the question, "Do cigarettes cause cancer?" Scientists from tobacco companies and doctors are certainly in disagreement over this issue. There is a warning on cigarette packaging; however, it does not say that cigarettes cause cancer. You may know many people who smoke who are cancer-free. Likewise, there are individuals that get lung cancer who never smoke.

Your job in reading these passages is to identify the problem (dependent variable) and determine the conflict of opinion over the cause (independent variable). Each scientist will provide you with data; some data will support only their respective position, and some data will support either position. Some data may attempt to discredit the data of the other scientist. You need to sort out these matters.

SCIENCE SKILLS REVIEW

EXERCISE 3

Presentation of Conflicting Viewpoints

DIRECTIONS: Read the descriptions of the following conflicting viewpoints and answer the accompanying questions. Answers are on page 205.

Two detectives are called to the scene of a crime at about 5:00 AM. The neighbors called police when they heard a noise at 4:30 AM; however, they thought it was a firecracker rather than a gun. The victim is a 25-year-old female with a gunshot wound to the head. There is a large bruise on the back of her head. The door to the apartment was locked and there is no sign of forced entry. Nothing appears to have been taken. There is a gun lying on the floor near the left hand of the woman. A check of the serial number found that the woman had recently purchased the weapon. There was a blood-soaked pillow just above the woman's head. The police could not find a suicide note. There did not appear to be any other physical evidence at the scene. Neighbors that were interviewed said that the woman had recently been divorced and that she had been noticeably upset by the divorce.

Detective I: Detective I believes that the death was a homicide and asks that the ex-husband to be picked up for questioning.

Detective II: Detective II believes that the death was a suicide and asks that the ex-husband be notified.

1. The dependent variable (the problem) is: _____
_____
_____.

2. The conflicting viewpoint is: _____
_____
_____.

3. The independent variable causing the conflict is: _____
_____
_____.

4. Fill in the following table:

Data	More Consistent with Detective I	More Consistent with Detective II	Equally Consistent with Both Detectives I and II
Gun Owned by Woman			
Bloody Pillow			
Bruise on Head			
Firecracker-Like Noise			
No Forced Entry			
Locked Door			
No Suicide Note			
Divorced Victim			
Despondent Victim			

STEP TWO

EXERCISE 4

Science Reasoning Passages

DIRECTIONS: Each passage is followed by several questions. After reading a passage, choose the best answer to each question. You may refer to the passages as often as necessary. Answers are on page 206.

PASSAGE I

Germination is the beginning of the growth of a seed after a period of inactivity. The following experiments were designed to compare the amount of time it takes for seeds of different vegetables to germinate.

Experiment 1: Radish seeds, soaked in water for 24 hours, were germinated at 25° C for 10 days. The results are shown in Graph 1.

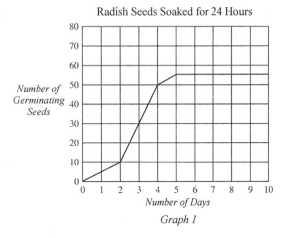

Graph 1

Experiment 2: Bean seeds, soaked in water for 24 hours, were germinated at 25° C for 10 days. The results are shown in Graph 2.

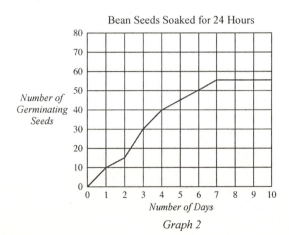

Graph 2

1. Graphs 1 and 2 show that after 3 days:

   A. more radish seeds have germinated.
   B. more bean seeds have germinated.
   C. equal numbers of radish seeds and bean seeds have germinated.
   D. no radish seeds or bean seeds have germinated.

2. A generalization that can be made about the data is that:

   F. 24 hours is the best soaking period for both radish seeds and bean seeds.
   G. radish seeds germinate more rapidly than bean seeds.
   H. the bean seeds had a steady rate of germination.
   J. most bean seeds of this kind require 7 days to germinate.

3. Which factor is the variable in this experiment?

   A. The period of the soaking
   B. The dishes in which the seeds were planted
   C. The rate of germination
   D. The kind of seeds used

4. To test the hypothesis that ultraviolet radiation affects bean seed germination, which of the following experimental designs would be best to use?

   F. Plant 20 normal bean seeds, note results; then plant 20 bean seeds that have been exposed to ultraviolet radiation, and compare results.
   G. Plant 20 bean seeds that have been exposed to ultraviolet radiation and at the same time plant 20 normal bean seeds, and compare the results.
   H. Use 20 radish seeds and 20 bean seeds that have been exposed to ultraviolet violation, and compare the results.
   J. Plant 50 bean seeds that have been exposed to ultraviolet radiation, and note the effects of the radiation.

PASSAGE II

A scientist wanted to determine the effects of different doses of an experimental drug called PCH. This drug was believed to help control weight gain. To test this hypothesis, four experimental groups, with 100 rats each, were given a dose every day with only sugar or a dose with sugar and a different amount of the drug. The rats were all fed the same kind and amount of food. After one year, the percentage of rats gaining weight was determined. The results of this experiment are presented in the following table.

Group	Contents of Dose	% of Rats Gaining Weight
1	5 grams of sugar	19%
2	5 grams of sugar 1 gram of PCH	21%
3	5 grams of sugar 5 grams of PCH	19%
4	5 grams of sugar 10 grams of PCH	20%

5. Which was the control group in this experiment?

   A. 1
   B. 2
   C. 3
   D. 4

6. As the dose of PCH increases, the percentage of rats gaining weight:

   F. increases.
   G. decreases.
   H. remains constant.
   J. varies.

7. In order to interpret the results of this experiment, it would be most useful to know the:

   A. characteristics of the rats in each group.
   B. chemical composition of PCH.
   C. kind of sugar used in the doses.
   D. kind of food fed to the rats.

8. From the data showing the percentage of rats gaining weight, it could be concluded that:

   F. PCH was effective in helping control the weight gain of the rats.
   G. sugar was required for the PCH to be effective.
   H. sugar alone was responsible for the weight gain of the rats.
   J. PCH had no significant effect in helping control the weight gain of the rats.

PASSAGE III

Atoms are considered the basic building blocks of matter. The atom consists of a positively charged center, or nucleus, surrounded by negatively charged electrons. The major kinds of particles in the nucleus are positively charged protons and neutrally charged neutrons. The number of protons, called the atomic number, identifies the element. The mass number of the atom represents the total number of protons and neutrons. Not all of the atoms of an element are identical. The different atoms of an element are called isotopes. The three carbon-isotopes are shown in the following table.

Name	Protons	Neutrons	Electrons	Mass Number
Carbon-12	6	6	6	12
Carbon-13	6	7	6	13
Carbon-14	6	8	6	14

9. The atomic number of the element carbon is:

   A. 6.
   B. 7.
   C. 12.
   D. 34.

10. The three carbon-isotopes all have:

    F. the same number of neutrons.
    G. the same mass number.
    H. an equal number of protons and electrons.
    J. an equal number of neutrons and protons.

11. Carbon-13 has:

    A. 6 protons and 7 electrons.
    B. 7 protons and 6 electrons.
    C. 6 protons and 7 neutrons.
    D. 13 protons.

12. If the isotope of an element contains 8 protons, 9 neutrons, and 8 electrons, the atomic number and mass number would be, respectively:

    F. 8 and 17.
    G. 9 and 17.
    H. 8 and 26.
    J. 9 and 26.

PASSAGE IV

Sodium chloride (table salt) is a crystal made up of rows of sodium (Na) ions and chloride (Cl) ions. Ions are atoms that are electrically charged. When sodium chloride is dissolved in water, it separates into its ions. The sodium ions and chloride ions are released from their positions in the crystal pattern and they move about freely. Other crystalline substances, such as sugar, do not produce ions when dissolved in water. When substances react with water to form ions, they are said to be ionized. The charged ions in the water are responsible for the conduction of electricity. Substances that conduct an electrical current when dissolved are called electrolytes. Substances that do not conduct an electric current are called non-electrolytes.

To study the electrical conductivity, an apparatus that measures the ability of substances to conduct electricity was used.

Experiment 1: Solid sodium chloride was tested and found to be a non-conductor. Pure water was also tested and found to be a non-conductor. When a teaspoon of sodium chloride was added to water, the solution was found to be a good conductor of electricity. Sugar did not conduct electricity as a solid or when dissolved in water.

Experiment 2: When a few crystals of sodium chloride were added to water, the solution showed a weak conduction of electricity. As additional sodium chloride was added, the ability of the solution to conduct electricity increased.

13. Experiment 1 indicates that sodium chloride conducts electricity when it:

    A. dissolves in alcohol.
    B. is tested as a solid.
    C. dissolves in water.
    D. is combined with sugar.

14. Which of the following graphs represents the relationship between the amount of sodium chloride dissolved in water and its conductivity?

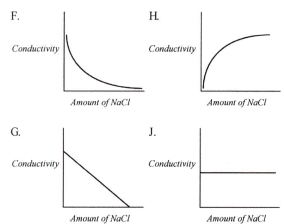

15. In order for a substance to be a conductor of electricity, the substance must have:

    A. rapidly moving molecules.
    B. charged particles that are free to move.
    C. ions in a crystalline form.
    D. been dissolved in a solvent.

16. Which of the following is not a characteristic of sugar?

    F. Solid sugar is an electrolyte.
    G. Solid sugar is a non-electrolyte.
    H. Solid sugar dissolves in water.
    J. Sugar solutions do not conduct electricity.

PASSAGE V

In the United States, there are millions of cases of food poisoning reported each year. Food poisoning is due to deadly bacteria, such as Salmonella. Since the mid-1980's, the United States Food and Drug Administration has approved irradiation of a variety of foods. Food is irradiated to destroy the harmful bacteria. During irradiation, gamma rays passing through food, break chemical bonds among atoms, and destroy the genetic material of the bacteria, preventing them from reproducing. Although the irradiation of food is becoming more widespread, the practice continues to be a controversial topic. The idea of an irradiated food supply is supported by some people and opposed by others.

Viewpoint 1: Proper preparation of food kills harmful bacteria in or on food. This means that irradiation is not necessary. According to some scientists, there is evidence that irradiation lessens the nutritional value of food by causing the loss of vitamins. Foods exposed to gamma rays have lost such vitamins as A, C, and E. One study found that animals that were fed irradiated food lost weight. Pregnant animals often miscarry, most likely due to reduced amounts of vitamin E in the irradiated food. Some chemicals in the food may be changed, resulting in the production of toxic by-products. While these unidentified toxic substances occur in small amounts, no one is certain what effect they will have as they accumulate in the body over a lifetime of consuming irradiated food.

Viewpoint 2: Food irradiation has significant value in destroying the bacteria that infect the food. Irradiated food has a much longer shelf life than traditionally treated food. Irradiation destroys nutrients but no more than is normally destroyed by cooking food. Food irradiated with 10,000 rads or less of gamma rays show little or no nutrient loss. According to the FDA, food exposed to greater than 10,000 rads exhibits nutrient loss that is generally no more than the loss that occurs in frozen and canned food. FDA scientists also admit that some by-products of the alteration of chemicals in the food are cancer-causing agents. However, they occurred in very small amounts in irradiated food. Most of these by-products turned out to be identical to naturally occurring food substances.

17. One of the principal differences between the viewpoints concerns:

    A. loss of nutritional value of food caused by irradiation.
    B. the effectiveness of food irradiation in destroying harmful bacteria.
    C. the accumulation of by-products of food irradiation in the body.
    D. the effect of gamma rays on the breakdown of vitamin A.

18. According to Viewpoint 1:

    F. the by-products of food irradiation are cancer-causing.
    G. the irradiation of food increases the nutritional value of food.
    H. the by-products of food irradiation are identical to naturally occurring food substances.
    J. the irradiation of food lessens the nutritional value of food.

19. These viewpoints are similar because they both suggest that food irradiation:

    A. is necessary to destroy harmful bacteria in food.
    B. is not necessary to destroy harmful bacteria in food.
    C. can lessen the nutritional value of food.
    D. can improve the nutritional value of food.

20. Which experimental information would NOT support Viewpoint 1?

    F. Food exposed to gamma rays loses much of vitamins A, C, and E.
    G. Food exposed to gamma rays does not lose much of vitamins A, C, and E.
    H. Toxic by-products of food alteration by gamma rays are accumulated in the body over a period of time.
    J. Irradiated food has a shelf life twice that of non-irradiated food.

PASSAGE VI

Nuclear reactors release great amounts of nuclear energy through controlled chain reactions. For this reason, nuclear power has been considered a source of abundant energy. Nuclear power, however, poses several problems. The most serious problem is the radioactive waste produced by the use of nuclear energy. The waste is very dangerous and remains so for thousands of years. How and where to dispose of this waste safely is a dilemma that has not been resolved. In 1987, the U.S. Congress authorized the Department of Energy to study Yucca Mountain in the southern desert of Utah as a place to bury the highly radioactive nuclear fuel rods from nuclear power plants.

Geologist 1: The most feasible and safe method for disposing of highly radioactive material is to store it underground. Yucca Mountain was chosen because it is believed that the mountain rock could keep the radioactive waste isolated for thousands of years. This proposed site is located underneath a thick layer of volcanic ash. It is above the ground water of aquifers in order to reduce the danger of seepage. The area is very remote and almost uninhabited. It is located in an area with low rainfall, thus less water enters the ground. It is also an area where the ground is mostly composed of volcanic tuff that slows down the filtration of water into the ground. The volcanic activity near Yucca Mountain is mild, with minimal chance for a large eruption. The chance of a severe earthquake is also remote.

Geologist 2: Burial of radioactive waste is the best disposal method. Yucca Mountain, however, is not the best site because it is hydrologically and geologically active. Burial at this site poses the risk of radioactive materials leaking out and contaminating surrounding soil and ground water. If a leak did occur, ground water contamination would be a major problem. Many of the surrounding cities, including parts of Las Vegas, receive some of their water from the aquifers in the area. The area around Yucca Mountain has numerous faults and even a small volcano nearby. Any significant geological activity could disturb waste containers. If earthquakes or volcanic eruptions occurred, the radioactive material at the site could be carried to the surface, threatening the entire region.

21. According to Geologist 1:

  A. radioactive waste should not be buried underground.
  B. the geologic structure of Yucca Mountain would minimize geological activity.
  C. earthquake or volcanic activity is likely to occur near Yucca Mountain.
  D. the radioactive waste should be buried somewhere other than Yucca Mountain.

22. Both geologists agree that:

  F. the radioactive waste should be buried somewhere other than Yucca Mountain.
  G. hydrological and geological activity near Yucca Mountain is minimal.
  H. the best way to store radioactive waste is burial underground.
  J. the radioactive waste is likely to leak into ground water.

23. Which of the following would provide the strongest evidence for the position of Geologist 2?

  A. The site is both geologically stable and safe from the entry of water.
  B. Construction at the site has been found to be destructive to animal habitats.
  C. The rock formations of Yucca Mountain will keep the waste sufficiently isolated for thousands of years.
  D. There is a periodic upwelling of ground water at Yucca Mountain.

24. Which of the following would provide the strongest evidence for the position of Geologist 1?

  F. The rock formations of Yucca Mountain were formed by rainwater seeping downward, not by groundwater seeping upward.
  G. There is a large aquifer underneath Yucca Mountain.
  H. The Yucca Mountain site is affected by 32 known earthquake faults.
  J. Rainwater containing nuclear chemicals has reached the site level.

STEP THREE: PROBLEM-SOLVING, CONCEPTS, AND STRATEGIES

ACT • PLAN • EXPLORE
SCIENCE REASONING

STEP THREE: PROBLEM-SOLVING, CONCEPTS, AND STRATEGIES

CAMBRIDGE COURSE CONCEPT OUTLINE

AMERICA'S #1 STANDARDS-BASED SCHOOL IMPROVEMENT

Cambridge Course Concept Outline
STEP THREE

I. ACT • PLAN • EXPLORE SCIENCE REASONING STEP THREE PROGRESS REPORTS (p. 55)

    A. ACT • PLAN EXPLORE SCIENCE REASONING STEP THREE STUDENT PROGRESS REPORT (p. 55)

    B. ACT • PLAN EXPLORE SCIENCE REASONING STEP THREE INSTRUCTOR PROGRESS REPORT (p. 57)

II. SECTION ONE—SCIENCE REASONING REVIEW (p. 61)

    A. SCIENCE REASONING PRELIMINARIES
1. OVERVIEW OF THE SCIENCE REASONING LESSON
2. FORMATS OF THE ACT, PLAN, AND EXPLORE SCIENCE REASONING TESTS
3. DIRECTIONS FOR SCIENCE REASONING PROBLEMS
4. WHAT IS TESTED

    B. THREE TYPES OF SCIENCE REASONING PASSAGES (p. 61)
1. DATA REPRESENTATION PASSAGES
   a. GRAPHS
      i. STRAIGHT LINES
      ii. PARABOLIC CURVES
      iii. GRAPH READING STRATEGIES (p. 61, Review Questions #1-3)
   b. TABLES (p. 62, Review Questions #4-9)
   c. TYPICAL DATA REPRESENTATION QUESTIONS (p. 64, Review Questions #10-14)
2. RESEARCH SUMMARY PASSAGES
   a. DESIGN QUESTIONS
   b. PREDICTION QUESTIONS
   c. EVALUATION QUESTIONS
   d. TYPICAL RESEARCH SUMMARY QUESTIONS (p. 66, Review Questions #15-25)
3. CONFLICTING VIEWPOINTS PASSAGES
   a. PREDICTION QUESTIONS
   b. "SPOT THE ASSUMPTIONS" QUESTIONS
   c. "PICK THE BEST ARGUMENT" QUESTIONS
   d. TYPICAL CONFLICTING VIEWPOINTS QUESTIONS (p. 69, Review Questions #26-36)

STEP THREE

C. THREE TYPES OF SCIENCE REASONING QUESTIONS
1. COMPREHENSION QUESTIONS
2. ANALYSIS QUESTIONS
3. APPLICATION QUESTIONS

D. STRATEGIES FOR THE SCIENCE REASONING TEST (p. 72)
1. GENERAL SCIENCE REASONING STRATEGIES
   a. PLAN YOUR ATTACK—EASIEST PASSAGES FIRST
   b. DO NOT PREVIEW QUESTION STEMS BEFORE READING PASSAGE
   c. UNDERLINE KEY WORDS AND PHRASES
   d. PAY ATTENTION TO WHAT IS THERE, NOT WHAT ISN'T
   e. PAY ATTENTION TO DIFFERENCES
   f. WATCH FOR ASSUMPTIONS
   g. LOOK FOR TRENDS
   h. TRANSCRIBE ANSWERS IN GROUPS
2. DATA REPRESENTATION STRATEGIES (p. 72, Review Questions #37-41)
3. RESEARCH SUMMARY STRATEGIES (p. 73, Review Questions #42-47)
4. CONFLICTING VIEWPOINTS STRATEGIES (p. 74, Review Questions #48-54)

III. SECTION TWO—SCIENCE REASONING PROBLEM-SOLVING (p. 76)

A. DATA REPRESENTATION PASSAGES (p. 76, Problem-Solving Questions #1-27)

B. RESEARCH SUMMARY PASSAGES (p. 81, Problem-Solving Questions #28-51)

C. CONFLICTING VIEWPOINTS PASSAGES (p. 88, Problem-Solving Questions #52-78)

IV. SECTION THREE—SCIENCE REASONING QUIZZES (p. 94)

A. QUIZ I (p. 94)

B. QUIZ II (p. 96)

C. QUIZ III (p. 98)

V. STRATEGY SUMMARY SHEET—SCIENCE REASONING (p. 102)

ACT • PLAN • EXPLORE SCIENCE REASONING
STEP THREE PROGRESS REPORT
(Student Copy)

DIRECTIONS: These progress reports are designed to help you monitor your ACT Science Reasoning Step Three progress. Complete the assigned problems corresponding to each lesson for Step Three, correct your answers, and record both the number and percentage of problems that you answered correctly. Identify the date on which you completed each exercise. List the numbers of any problems that you would like your instructor to review in class.

Transfer this information to the Instructor Copy, and then give that report to your instructor.

Name _____ Student ID _____ Date _____

ACT • PLAN • EXPLORE SCIENCE REASONING
(Student Copy)

Section	Total # Possible	Assigned	# Correct	% Correct	Date Completed	Problem #s to Review
1. Science Reasoning Review (p. 61)	54					
2. Science Reasoning Problem-Solving (p. 76)	78					
3. Science Reasoning Quiz 1 (p. 94)	10					
4. Science Reasoning Quiz 2 (p. 96)	10					
5. Science Reasoning Quiz 3 (p. 98)	11					

ACT • PLAN • EXPLORE SCIENCE REASONING
STEP THREE PROGRESS REPORT
(Instructor Copy)

DIRECTIONS: Transfer the information from your Student Copy to the Instructor Copy below. Leave the last three bolded columns blank. Your instructor will use them to evaluate your progress. When finished, give these reports to your instructor.

Student Name _____ Student ID _____ Date _____

ACT • PLAN • EXPLORE SCIENCE REASONING
(Instructor Copy)

Section	Total # Possible	Assigned	# Correct	% Correct	Date Completed	Problem #s to Review	Mastered	Partially Mastered	Not Mastered
1. Science Reasoning Review (p. 61)	54								
2. Science Reasoning Problem-Solving (p. 76)	78								
3. Science Reasoning Quiz 1 (p. 94)	10								
4. Science Reasoning Quiz 2 (p. 96)	10								
5. Science Reasoning Quiz 3 (p. 98)	11								

Instructor Skill Evaluation (Check One Per Section) applies to the last three columns.

ACT • PLAN • EXPLORE
SCIENCE REASONING

SCIENCE REASONING REVIEW, PROBLEM-SOLVING, AND QUIZZES

SECTION ONE—SCIENCE REASONING REVIEW

DIRECTIONS: The questions in this section accompany the review of the concepts and skills tested by the ACT, PLAN, and EXPLORE Science Reasoning Tests. Each passage is followed by several questions. After reading a passage, choose the best answer to each question. You may refer to the passages as often as necessary. You are NOT permitted to use a calculator. Answers are on page 207.

Passage I

The kinetic energy of an object with mass m (measured in grams) after a fall from a height h (measured in centimeters) was recorded for different heights. A graph was made representing the kinetic energy versus height.

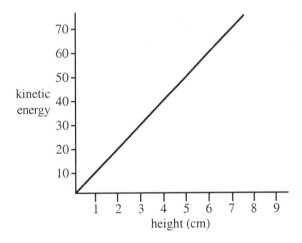

1. If the kinetic energy is given in units of $g \cdot cm^2/s^2$, what units must the slope have?

    A. $g \cdot cm/s$
    B. $g \cdot cm/s^2$
    C. $s \cdot cm/g$
    D. $s^2/(g \cdot cm)$

2. It is discovered that if we redo the experiment with an object with twice the mass, the kinetic energy obtained for every height is doubled. The slope of the new set of experiments can be obtained by doing what to the old slope?

    F. Multiplying by 2
    G. Dividing by 2
    H. Squaring
    J. Taking the square root

3. What would be the kinetic energy in $g \cdot cm^2/s^2$ of an object of mass m if it were dropped from a height of 4.5 cm?

    A. 4.5
    B. 9.0
    C. 45
    D. 90

Passage II

A scientist investigated the variables that affect the age at which a female of the animal species *taedi periculum* first gives birth. Some of the results of this study are summarized in the table below.

Experiment	Temperature (° C)	Average food intake (grams)	Age when first gave birth (months)
1	25	15	7
2	25	30	6
3	25	45	4
4	35	15	5
5	35	30	3
6	35	45	3

4. Which of the following would be good animals to use for the experiment?

   F. Adult females
   G. Newborn females
   H. Newborn males
   J. Adult males

5. Which of the pairs of experiments listed below would be useful for studying the effect of temperature on the age of first birth?

   A. 1 and 2
   B. 1 and 5
   C. 1 and 4
   D. 2 and 6

6. If all other variables are kept constant, which of the following will result in an increase in the age at which the animals give birth?

   F. Increase in temperature from 25° C to 35° C
   G. Increase in food from 15 grams to 45 grams
   H. Decrease in food from 30 grams to 15 grams
   J. Increase in temperature from 25° C to 30° C

7. Which experiment was the control for temperature for Experiment 5?

   A. Experiment 1
   B. Experiment 2
   C. Experiment 3
   D. Experiment 6

8. If an experiment was set up with the temperature set at 30° C and the food intake at 30 grams, which of the following would be a reasonable prediction of the age in months of the animals when they first gave birth?

   F. 7.5
   G. 6.0
   H. 4.5
   J. 2.5

9. Which of the following conclusions is consistent with the data presented in the table?

   A. The weight of the firstborn is proportional to the food intake.
   B. The weight of the firstborn is related to the temperature.
   C. The age of the mother at time of first offspring's birth increases with decreasing food intake.
   D. The age of the mother at time of first offspring's birth decreases with decreasing food intake.

NOTES AND STRATEGIES

Passage III

The chart below shows the average blood pressure and relative total surface area associated with the different types of human blood vessels.

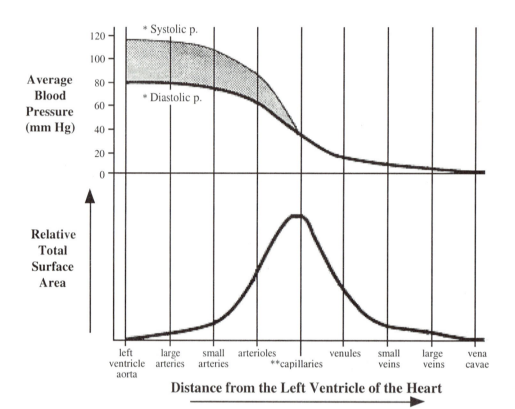

*Pulse is the difference <u>between</u> systolic and diastolic pressure.
**Blood velocity is lowest in the capillaries (averaging 3 cm/sec.).

10. According to the diagram, pulse pressure can be detected:

   F. in large arteries only.
   G. in large arteries as well as in large veins.
   H. in blood vessels between the aorta and the capillaries.
   J. primarily in the arterioles, capillaries, and venules.

11. Based on the information in the diagram, which of the following conclusions about average blood pressure is correct?

   A. The average blood pressure decreases continuously as it gets further away from the left ventricle.
   B. The average blood pressure remains approximately the same as it passes through the different blood vessels of the body.
   C. Starting at the aorta, average blood pressure first increases and then decreases.
   D. The average blood pressure is highest in the blood vessels with the greatest relative total surface area.

12. Which of the following correctly states the relationship between the relative total surface area of different blood vessels and their average blood pressure?

    F. As relative total surface area decreases, average blood pressure increases.
    G. As relative total surface area decreases, average blood pressure decreases.
    H. As relative total surface area decreases, average blood pressure may increase or decrease.
    J. Average blood pressure always changes in the opposite direction as the relative total surface area changes.

13. Which of the following conclusions can be drawn from the information provided in the diagram?

    A. As the distance of blood vessels from the left ventricle increases, their relative total surface area decreases.
    B. As the distance of blood vessels from the left ventricle increases, their pulse pressure increases.
    C. Blood vessels with the greatest relative total surface area have the highest pulse pressure.
    D. Blood vessels closest to and farthest away from the left ventricle have the smallest relative total surface area.

14. A physician examining a newly discovered tribe of people deep in the Amazon jungles found that the relative total surface area of their capillaries was greater than that previously reported for any other group of people. If the physician were to predict the average velocity of blood through the capillaries of these people, which of the following values would be most reasonable?

    F. 2 cm/sec
    G. 3 cm/sec
    H. 4 cm/sec
    J. 5 cm/sec

Passage IV

To test the hypothesis that all antibiotics are equally effective in preventing bacterial growth, the following three experiments were carried out using clear plastic plates filled with nutrient agar (a mixture of ingredients that supports the growth of bacteria).

Experiment 1: Three plates (A, B, and C) of agar were set up, each with an equal amount of bacterial culture (Bacterium X) spread over the agar surface and with a paper disk placed in the center. Plate A's disk was soaked in Antibiotic I; Plate B's disk was soaked in Antibiotic II; Plate C's disk was soaked in plain water. After incubation overnight at 37° C (body temperature), Plates A and B had a clear area, 2" in diameter surrounding the paper disk, but beyond this 2" region, the plates were cloudy. Plate C was entirely cloudy, including the area adjacent to the paper disk. When bacteria reproduce successfully, colonies form on the agar, giving it a cloudy appearance.

Experiment 2: Identical procedures were followed except that Plates A, B, and C were incubated overnight at 22° C (room temperature). After incubation, Plate A had a clear area, 2" in diameter, surrounding the paper disk. Plates B and C were entirely cloudy.

Experiment 3: Identical procedures were followed except that the concentrations of Antibiotic I (Plate A) and Antibiotic II (Plate B) were made twice as strong. After incubation overnight at 22° C, Plates A and B both had clear, 2" areas around the paper disk, while Plate C remained entirely cloudy.

15. After incubation, a clear area around a previously soaked paper disk represents a region where:

    A. agar had washed away.
    B. decomposition had occurred due to high incubation temperatures.
    C. bacterial growth did not occur.
    D. bacteria grew best.

16. Which of the following results would indicate that the antibiotics being tested have nothing to do with the control of bacterial growth?

    F. A clear, 2" region was always observed around the disks soaked in water.
    G. All results remained the same at the two experimental temperatures and at the two antibiotic concentration levels.
    H. Plates A and B always remained clear.
    J. The disks soaked in water were not used in the experiments at all.

17. Which statement is supported by the results of Experiment 1 alone?

    A. Antibiotic I, Antibiotic II, and water are equally effective as inhibitors (preventers) of bacterial growth at 37° C.
    B. Dry paper disks can be effective in controlling bacterial growth at 37° C.
    C. The concentration of an antibiotic may influence its effectiveness in controlling bacterial growth at 37° C.
    D. Both Antibiotics I and II can inhibit bacterial growth at 37° C.

18. The results of both Experiment 2 and Experiment 3 lead to which of the following conclusions?

    F. Antibiotics I and II have similar effects on bacterial growth, regardless of concentrations.
    G. Antibiotic II and water have similar effects on bacterial growth, regardless of concentrations.
    H. The effectiveness of Antibiotic I at 22° C depends on its concentration.
    J. The effectiveness of Antibiotic II at 22° C depends on its concentration.

19. Which hypothesis best explains the observation that the agar plates never appear clear beyond a 2" area surrounding the soaked paper disks?

    A. The bacteria cannot grow well within 2" of any moist paper disks.
    B. The antibiotics cannot seep through the agar beyond a distance of 2".
    C. At the experimental incubation temperatures used, the two antibiotics interfere with each other's effectiveness.
    D. The paper disks can absorb nutrients out of the agar from the distance of 2".

20. If either Antibiotic I or II could be prescribed for internal use to prevent the spread of Bacterium X infections, which recommendation, based on the experimental results, is appropriate if the cost due to the amount of antibiotic used per dose is the most critical factor (the antibiotics are equal in cost for equal concentrations)?

    F. Either Antibiotic I or II can be taken at equal cost.
    G. Antibiotic I would be less expensive.
    H. Antibiotic II would be less expensive.
    J. Neither Antibiotic I nor II would be effective in preventing the spread of Bacterium X.

NOTES AND STRATEGIES

Passage V

To investigate the hypothesis that the quality of the detail of a fossil depends on the size of the particles that make up the rock surrounding the fossil, three experiments were performed using a particular type of leaf with many fine veins.

Experiment 1: A leaf was placed on a flat bed made of paste from extra-fine plaster and then completely covered with more of the same paste. A glass cover with a 5-lb weight was placed on top of the paste for one hour, until the plaster set. The plaster was then baked for 30 minutes at 25° C. When the cast was opened, the imprint of the leaf showed all of the veins, including the finest ones.

Experiment 2: A leaf was placed on a flat bed made of paste from fine-grade plaster and then completely covered with more of the same paste. A glass cover with a 5-lb weight was placed on top of the plaster for one hour, until the plaster set. The plaster was then baked for 30 minutes at 25° C. When the cast was opened, all the main veins were visible, but only isolated traces of the finer veins were found.

Experiment 3: A leaf was placed on a flat bed made of paste from coarse-grain plaster and then completely covered with more of the same paste. A glass cover with a 5-lb weight was placed on top of the plaster for one hour, until the plaster set. The plaster was then baked for 30 minutes at 25° C. When the cast was opened, only the thickest veins were visible, and some of the leaf edge was difficult to discern.

21. Should the investigator have used a different type of leaf in each experiment?

    A. Yes: different types of structure could be studied.
    B. Yes: in real life, many different types of fossils are found.
    C. No: the leaf served as a controlled variable.
    D. No: the nature of the leaf is not important.

22. When a fossil is formed, the sediment that surrounds it is normally compressed by the tons of earth deposited over it. What part of the model simulates this compressing element?

    F. The 5-lb weight
    G. The glass
    H. The upper layer of paste
    J. The baking oven

23. A fourth experiment was set up the same way as the previous three, except the paste was made by mixing equal amounts of very coarse sand with the extra-fine plaster. The investigator is likely to discover:

    A. no change from Experiment 1 because only the plaster counts.
    B. no change because the same kind of leaf is used.
    C. the imprint is better than Experiment 1 because the sand provides air pockets.
    D. the imprint is worse than Experiment 1 because the average particle size is bigger.

24. Which of the following hypotheses is supported by the results of Experiment 1 alone?

    F. The finer the sediment the greater the detail of the resulting fossil.
    G. Hardened sediment can preserve the imprint of a specimen.
    H. All fossils must have been baked at high temperatures.
    J. Only organic material can leave imprints in sediment.

25. Which of the following changes in the experiments would have permitted a test of the hypothesis that the quality of a fossil imprint depends on the pressure applied?

    A. Repeat the experiments except for using a 10-lb weight in Experiment 2, and a 20-lb weight in Experiment 3.
    B. Choose one of the plasters, and run experiments using the same plaster in all trials while varying the weights.
    C. Rerun all the experiments without the glass.
    D. Vary the depth of the leaf in each new trial, because in nature increased pressure means the fossil is at a greater depth.

Passage VI

Theory 1: Early in the twentieth century, many chemists believed that the stability of the molecule methane, CH_4, could be explained by the "octet" rule, which states that stability occurs when the central atom, in this case carbon, is surrounded by eight "valence," or outer, electrons. Four of these originally came from the outer electrons of the carbon itself, and four came from the four surrounding hydrogen atoms (the hydrogen atom was considered an exception to the rule since it was known to favor a closed shell of two electrons as helium has.) According to the octet rule, neither CH_3 nor CH_5 should exist as stable compounds, and this prediction has been borne out by experiment.

Theory 2: While the octet rule predicted many compounds accurately, it also had shortcomings. Ten electrons, for example, surround the compound PC_{l5}. The greatest shock to the octet rule concerned noble gases such as krypton and xenon, which have eight electrons surrounding them in their atomic states, and therefore should not form compounds since no more electrons would be needed to make an octet. The discovery in 1960 that xenon could form compounds such as XeF_4 forced consideration of a new theory, which held that (a) compounds formed when electrons were completely paired, either in bonds or in non-bonded pairs; (b) the total number of shared electrons around a central atom varied, and could be as high as twelve; (c) the shapes of compounds were such as to keep the pairs of electrons as far from each other as possible.

For example, since six electrons in the atomic state surround sulfur, in the compound SF_6 it acquired six additional shared electrons from the surrounding fluorines for a total of twelve electrons. The shape of the compound is "octahedral," as shown below, since this conformation minimizes the overlap of bonding pairs of electrons.

26. According to Theory 1, the compound CH_2Cl_2:

    F. should have eight electrons surrounding the carbon atom.
    G. cannot exist since the original carbon atom does not have eight electrons.
    H. should have eight electrons surrounding each hydrogen atom.
    J. requires more electrons for stability.

27. According to Theory 1, the compound XeF_4:

    A. exists with an octet structure around the xenon.
    B. should not exist since more than eight electrons surround the xenon.
    C. will have similar chemical properties to CH_4.
    D. exists with the xenon surrounded by twelve electrons.

28. The atom boron has three outer electrons, and in bonding to boron, a fluorine atom donates one electron. The BF_3 molecule is known to exist. Which of the following is true?

    F. BF_3 obeys Theory 1.
    G. The existence of BF_3 contradicts Theory 2.
    H. According to Theory 2, the structure of BF_3 is a pyramid:

    J. According to Theory 2, the structure of BF_3 is triangular and planar:

29. A scientist seeking to explain why Theory 2 has more predictive power than Theory 1 might argue that:

    A. eight electrons shall represent a "closed shell."
    B. while eight electrons represent a "closed shell" for some atoms, for others the closed shell may be six, ten, or twelve.
    C. it is incorrect to assume that a given atom always has the same number of electrons around it.
    D. CH_4 is not as important a compound as XeF_4.

30. Theory 2 could be threatened by evidence of:

    F. the existence of SF_4.
    G. the existence of XeF_5.
    H. molecules with stable octets.
    J. the existence of SF_6.

Passage VII

Scientist 1: The atmosphere of the Earth was at one time almost totally lacking in oxygen. One piece of evidence supporting this assertion is the very fact that life got started at all. The first chemical reactions that are necessary for the origin of life, the formation of amino acids, require ultraviolet light. Most of the ultraviolet light coming from the Sun is now absorbed by oxygen in the atmosphere. If there were as much oxygen in the atmosphere then as there is now, there would have been too little ultraviolet light available to enable life to begin. Also, the oldest bacteria, the ones that have the shortest DNA, are almost all anaerobes—they either do not need oxygen or die if exposed to oxygen. Most of the oxygen that exists now entered the atmosphere later from volcanic fumes.

Scientist 2: The prevailing opinion is that the atmosphere, though thicker now than it was in the past, is not essentially different in composition. The argument that the Earth must originally have been deficient in oxygen is flawed. First of all, the presence of iron and other oxides in the rocks from this time indicates that there was oxygen available. Secondly, the requirement for a great deal of ultraviolet light holds only if there is a low concentration of the starting materials in the water. If the water in some prehistoric lake began to freeze, the starting materials would be concentrated in a small volume of unfrozen water. The high concentration of the starting materials would offset the so-called deficiency of ultraviolet light, and life could begin.

31. According to the hypothesis of Scientist 1, which of the following would have been among the last living things to evolve?

    A. Anaerobes
    B. Plants
    C. Insects
    D. Viruses

32. According to the information presented by Scientist 1, if his theory of the origin of oxygen in the atmosphere is correct, the total amount of oxygen in the air over the next million years, on the average, should:

    F. decrease, then increase.
    G. increase, then decrease.
    H. increase.
    J. decrease.

33. Underlying the argument of Scientist 2 is the assumption that the oxygen in the oxides in the rocks was:

    A. always tied up in the rocks.
    B. involved in biological reactions.
    C. all gaseous during the early days of the atmosphere.
    D. proportional to the oxygen in the atmosphere at the time.

34. Underlying Scientist 1's suggestion that the evolutionary record supports the idea of an oxygen deficiency on the early Earth is the assumption that the oldest living things:

    F. have the shortest DNA.
    G. have the most fragmented DNA.
    H. have changed radically.
    J. must have died out.

35. Which of the following is the strongest argument Scientist 1 could use to counter Scientist 2's suggested mechanism for the origin of life?

    A. There was not enough ultraviolet light available.
    B. Chemical reactions occurred differently then.
    C. The temperature at the surface of the Earth at that time was always above 35° C because of geothermal heat release.
    D. Most lakes would not have covered large enough areas to guarantee that all the essential building blocks were present.

36. To refute Scientist 1's hypothesis, Scientist 2 might best show that:

    F. the amount of oxide in rocks has changed little over the past four billion years.
    G. there are ways of making the biologically important molecules without ultraviolet light.
    H. there are complex anaerobic bacteria.
    J. the atmospheric pressure has not changed over the Earth's history.

NOTES AND STRATEGIES

Passage VIII

Ocean water contains "salt"—actually a mixture of ions, primarily sodium, chloride, potassium, calcium, magnesium, bicarbonate, and sulfate. The solid-line graph below indicates the percentage of these ions ("salinity") in a slab of ice that lies over seawater on a cold ocean surface. The arrow and dashed line indicate the salinity of the water beneath the ice.

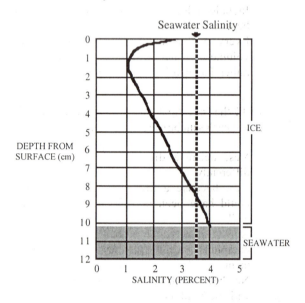

37. According to this figure, the salt content of the ice above the ocean water:

    A. equals 0.
    B. is constant at all depths.
    C. generally decreases with greater depth.
    D. generally increases with greater depth.

38. Compared to the ocean water below it, the salinity of the ice is:

    F. generally lower.
    G. about the same.
    H. generally higher.
    J. unable to be determined.

39. The salinity of the ice at the surface of the slab is equal to the salinity of:

    A. the ice at a depth of approximately 1.5 cm.
    B. the ice at a depth of approximately 7.0 cm.
    C. the ice at a depth of approximately 9.0 cm.
    D. the water beneath the ice.

40. An experimenter wants to take a sample of ice that is one half the salinity of the seawater below. At what depth should he sample?

    F. Between 1 and 2 cm
    G. Between 4 and 5 cm
    H. Either between 0 and 1 cm or between 3 and 4 cm
    J. Between 5 and 6 cm

41. The investigator takes a 1-gram sample of ice from a depth of 10 cm, and wishes to take a sample of ice from 1.3 cm depth that will contain the same weight of total salts. How large a sample is needed?

    A. 0.25 grams
    B. 1.0 grams
    C. 4.0 grams
    D. 10 grams

Passage IX

Erosion refers to processes that wear down rocks and soil, as well as processes that transport the worn-away materials to other locations. Although these processes usually cause effects gradually (over geologic time), laboratory models can be designed to investigate which environmental factors affect erosion rate.

Three experimental sandboxes were set up that were identical in size (10 ft. • 15 ft.), had identical types of soil and rocks, and were filled to equal depths (3 ft.). The sandboxes were kept for two weeks in large environmental chambers, each maintained at a constant temperature, with a continuous wind flow of 5 mph.

Sandbox 1: One half was kept bare (just soil and rocks), while the other half had a variety of grasses and weeds planted among the soil and rocks. After two weeks, the bare half had small channels (ruts) running along its length that averaged 1 inch in width. The planted half had few channels, and those that were found averaged less than 1 inch wide.

Sandbox 2: The conditions were identical to those of Sandbox 1, with the addition that both halves were subjected to light, 15-minute showers of water every twelve hours. After two weeks, the bare half had channels averaging 4 inches wide, while the planted half had fewer channels averaging 2 inches wide.

Sandbox 3: The conditions were identical to those of Sandbox 2, but the entire box was mechanically raised to rest at an angle of 15° to simulate a steep slope. After two weeks, the bare half had channels averaging 7 inches wide, while channels in the planted half were less common and averaged 4 inches in width.

42. Results from all three sandboxes indicate that:

    F. different types of soils and rocks are affected differently by environmental factors.
    G. under all tested conditions, plants reduce erosion.
    H. changing wind and temperature conditions can affect erosion patterns.
    J. water from short periods of rain has little or no effect on erosion patterns.

43. Which of the following claims does the design and results of the experiments NOT support?

    A. Light winds have no erosive effect.
    B. Slopes have more erosion than level surfaces.
    C. Water has major erosive effects.
    D. The effects of changing temperature remain unanswered.

44. Sudden cloudbursts are known to cause more erosion than longer periods of mild rains. How could the present experiments be changed to examine this idea?

    F. Raise the angle in Sandbox 3 to produce a steeper slope.
    G. Add the "rain conditions" from Sandbox 2 to the conditions in Sandbox 1.
    H. Include light, 15-minute showers every six hours instead of every twelve hours.
    J. Every twelve hours allow the same total volume of water to fall in a 5-minute span rather than in a 15-minute span.

45. Should the investigator have used different soil types in each sandbox experiment?

    A. Yes, because different soils may erode differently.
    B. Yes, because a different group of plants could have been used in each sandbox as well.
    C. No, because some soils can be washed completely away within the 2-week experiment.
    D. No, because the soil type was a controlled variable in all three experiments.

46. Sandbox 3 specifically demonstrates the role of which particular variable in the set of experiments?

    F. Rain
    G. Wind
    H. Gravity
    J. Temperature

47. If another sandbox were set up, which of the following conditions would probably cause wider and deeper channels in the soil of the new sandbox than those in Sandbox 3?

    I. Steeper angles for the sandbox
    II. A greater volume of water during the 15-minute showers every twelve hours
    III. Removal of plants from soil

    A. I only
    B. I and II only
    C. II and III only
    D. I, II, and III

Passage X

In the 1940s, 1950s, and 1960s, the growing field of animal behavior maintained an ongoing debate about the origin of observed behavior in many different animal species. Two extreme viewpoints were at the center of this "Nature vs. Nurture" debate.

Viewpoint 1 (Nature): Many behaviors or instincts are literally programmed by one or more genes. Genes serve as "blueprints" that enable an individual to carry out a particular stereotyped behavior (Fixed Action Pattern) as soon as the appropriate stimulus (releaser) is observed. Other individuals do not have to be observed performing the behavior. The releasing stimulus need never have been seen before. At first view of the releaser and every time thereafter, the Fixed Action Pattern will be carried out to completion in the exact same way—even if the releaser is removed before the Fixed Action Pattern is finished! Examples include: a) the pecking of baby gulls at the red spot on their mother's bill (which causes the mother gull to regurgitate food), b) song birds producing their species song without ever having heard it before, and c) a male stickle-back fish defending its territory by attacking anything red because other breeding males always have red underbellies.

Viewpoint 2 (Nurture): Many behaviors are determined by experience and/or learning during an individual's lifetime. Genes provide the limits of the "blank slate" that each individual starts out as, but then various experiences will determine the actual behavior patterns within the individual genetic range of possibilities. In other words, behavior can be modified. Examples include: a) positive ("reward") reinforcement and punishment causing a behavior to increase and decrease (respectively), and b) songbirds producing their species song only after having heard it performed by other individuals of their species.

48. The red spot on a mother gull's bill is called a(n):

    F. Fixed Action Pattern.
    G. instinct.
    H. releaser.
    J. stereotyped response.

49. To refute the strict "genetic blueprint" ideas of Viewpoint 1, a scientist could show that:

    A. baby gulls peck at a stick with a red spot.
    B. baby gulls will peck at mother gulls' red spot as soon as they hatch out of their eggs.
    C. baby gulls pecking at the red spot happens exactly the same way each time.
    D. baby gulls' accuracy in pecking at mother gulls' red spot improves with practice.

50. A food-seeking blue jay captured a distinctively colored butterfly that had a bad-tasting substance in its tissues. After spitting out the butterfly, it never again tried to capture a similarly colored butterfly. This incident seems to support:

    F. Viewpoint 1.
    G. Viewpoint 2.
    H. both viewpoints.
    J. neither viewpoint (the incident is irrelevant).

51. Which of the following supports Viewpoint 1?

    A. A rat reaches the end of a maze by the same route, but finishes faster after each trip.
    B. Monkey A watches other monkeys wash sweet potatoes before they eat them; then, he washes sweet potatoes before he eats them.
    C. A male stickleback fish attacks a picture of a red mailbox held in front of his aquarium.
    D. A bird performs its species song after hearing the song only once.

52. If baby chickens peck at grains of food on the ground when hungry, but not as much after they have recently eaten, then this:

    F. supports Viewpoint 1.
    G. supports Viewpoint 2.
    H. does not refer to behavior.
    J. is irrelevant to the Nature vs. Nurture debate.

53. It is thought that some species of birds "learn" to fly. This belief is based on observations of young birds fluttering and flapping their wings at the nest until they reach the age when flight is possible. In Species X, nestlings were kept in harmless, but tight plastic tubes in which they could not carry out such "practice movements." They were released when they reached the age of flight. Viewpoint 1 predicts that the birds will fly:

    A. after fluttering their wings for a time.
    B. after watching other birds flutter their wings.
    C. after watching other birds flutter and fly.
    D. immediately.

54. A songbird can sing its species song after it hears other birds of its own species singing. Yet, if it hears the song from another species, the bird will not sing the "foreign" song. This suggests that:

    F. genetic "programming" and experience play a role in this species' ability to sing its song.
    G. this species' song is a Fixed Action Pattern.
    H. song development in this species is strictly a learned behavior with no genetic component.
    J. genes appear to be far more important than experience in this example.

NOTES AND STRATEGIES

STEP THREE

SECTION TWO—SCIENCE REASONING PROBLEM-SOLVING

DIRECTIONS: The questions in this section reflect both the format and difficulty range of problems on the ACT Science Reasoning Test. Each passage is followed by several questions. After reading a passage, choose the best answer to each question. You may refer to the passages as often as necessary. You are NOT permitted to use a calculator. Answers are on page 207.

Passage I

The graph of the thin line below shows the hearing sensitivity of female moths. The auditory characteristics of certain sounds important to moth survival are also included.

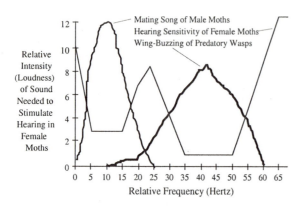

1. According to the graph, female moths are most sensitive to sounds between:

    A. 0-5 Hertz.
    B. 5-15 Hertz.
    C. 20-25 Hertz.
    D. 35-50 Hertz.

2. The nervous system of female moths may be set up to allow them to respond differently to sounds of different frequencies. Based on the information in the graph, which statement best describes the appropriate responses of female moths?

    F. Approach sounds between 5-15 Hertz, withdraw from sounds between 35-50 Hertz
    G. Approach sounds between 35-50 Hertz, withdraw from sounds between 5-15 Hertz
    H. Approach sounds between 5-15 Hertz and 35-50 Hertz
    J. Withdraw from sounds between 5-15 Hertz and 35-50 Hertz

3. Which of the following statements is supported by the information in the graph?

    A. The wing-buzzing sounds of wasps occur at a narrower range of frequencies than the range of the male moth mating song.
    B. The frequency range of the male moth mating song is narrower than the range of wasp wing-buzzing sounds.
    C. Female moths cannot hear sounds with relative intensities less than 3.
    D. Male moths are less sensitive to sounds than predatory wasps.

4. Which of the following statements accurately describes the relationship between the male moth mating song and female moth hearing sensitivity?

    F. The frequency range of the male song coincides with the frequency range at which females are maximally sensitive to any sound.
    G. Females need not be maximally sensitive at the frequency range of the male song because of the extremely high intensity of the song.
    H. Females cannot hear the male song if its intensity level is less than 10.
    J. The male song does not extend to an intensity level above 10.

5. If a new species of wasp were introduced into the moths' environment, which of the following wing-buzzing characteristics would make it the most successful predator of female moths?

    A. Extremely high intensity at relative frequencies between 35-50 Hertz
    B. An intensity level of 7-8 at relative frequencies between 20-25 Hertz
    C. Low intensity at relative frequencies above 60 Hertz
    D. Extremely high intensity at relative frequencies above 60 Hertz

6. A "new male" comes to town having a mating song with a frequency range between 20-25 Hertz and an intensity level of 4. What are his chances of finding a mate?

    F. Excellent
    G. Poor
    H. Good, if no wasps are present
    J. Cannot be determined from the given information

Passage II

Graph I shows the relationship between the relative rates of activity of enzymes A and B and temperature. Graph II shows the relationship between the relative rates of activity of enzymes A and B and pH.

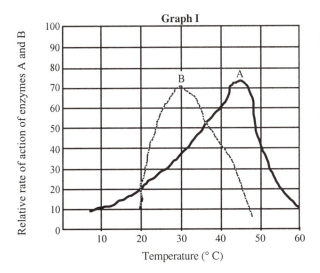
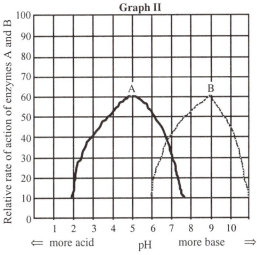

7. Under which conditions is enzyme A most effective?

   A. 40° C and a pH of 5
   B. 45° C and a pH of 5
   C. 45° C and a pH of 9
   D. 50° C and a pH of 9

8. The optimum environment for enzyme B is:

   F. acidic.
   G. basic.
   H. either acidic or basic.
   J. neutral.

9. At which one of the following temperatures do A and B exhibit the same relative rate of action?

   A. 6.9° C
   B. 10° C
   C. 37° C
   D. 47° C

10. At which pH do both A and B exhibit the same relative rate of action?

    F. 6.9
    G. 10
    H. 37
    J. 47

11. At what temperature does A have half the activity of B?

    A. 20° C
    B. 25° C
    C. 42° C
    D. 53° C

12. At what temperature does B have half the activity of A?

    F. 20° C
    G. 30° C
    H. 42° C
    J. 53° C

13. Over which of the following pH ranges will both A and B be active?

    A. 1 to 3
    B. 3 to 6
    C. 6 to 8
    D. 8 to 10

14. At what pH will both A and B be at their maximum activity?

    F. 2
    G. 5
    H. 8.5
    J. No such pH

Passage III

A seismographic station can detect how far away an earthquake occurred, but it cannot determine the direction of the earthquake. Any given station can therefore report that the epicenter of an Earthquake occurred somewhere on the circumference of a circle. The map below shows the data recorded for an earthquake at three different seismic stations (A, B, and C). Intersections of the three seismic stations' curves are marked by Roman numerals.

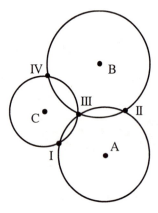

15. Which station was closest to the earthquake epicenter?

    A. A
    B. B
    C. C
    D. Cannot be determined from the given information

16. Given the information from stations A and B only, which site(s) is (are) possible for the earthquake epicenter?

    F. I only
    G. III only
    H. II and III only
    J. I and III only

17. Given the information from stations A and C only, which site(s) is (are) possible for the earthquake epicenter?

    A. I only
    B. III only
    C. II and III only
    D. I and III only

18. Given the information from all three stations, which site(s) is (are) possible for the epicenter?

    F. I only
    G. III only
    H. I and III only
    J. II and III only

19. If a fourth seismic station gave a report, at what point must its curve meet A's curve?

    A. I
    B. II
    C. III
    D. IV

20. If a fourth seismic station gave a report, at what point must its curve meet C's curve?

    F. I
    G. II
    H. III
    J. IV

21. What is the minimum number of points where two circumferences from two seismic stations, both measuring the same Earthquake, can meet?

    A. 1
    B. 2
    C. 3
    D. Infinite

NOTES AND STRATEGIES

STEP THREE

Passage IV

A scientist investigated the number of fossils per cubic foot through several feet in a quarry. The results are presented below.

Layer	Fish	Shells	Plants	Land Reptile
1 (TOP)	0	0	3	1
2	0	1	8	2
3	1	10	4	0
4	5	18	1	0
5	7	20	0	0

22. When was the site most likely above water?

    F. During the formation of Layers 1 and 2
    G. During the formation of Layers 2 and 3
    H. During the formation of Layers 1 and 4
    J. During the formation of Layer 3

23. Was the site most recently above or below water?

    A. Above
    B. Below
    C. Borderline
    D. Cannot be determined from the given information

24. What assumption is made to relate the fossil record to the environment?

    F. No assumption
    G. That fossils do not affect the environment
    H. That the fossils are mostly from plants and animals that lived in the region
    J. That only animal fossils are important

25. No trilobite fossils were found. This proves:

    A. that no trilobites were in the region.
    B. that the layers were formed before trilobites existed.
    C. that the layers were formed after the trilobites died out.
    D. nothing about the presence of the trilobite in the region.

26. A nautilus shell was found in Layer 3. This proves that:

    F. Layer 3 formed while the nautilus still existed.
    G. Layer 3 is newer than Layer 2.
    H. Layer 3 is older than Layer 2.
    J. the nautilus once lived on land.

27. Where will the newest layer form?

    A. Under Layer 4
    B. Over Layer 1
    C. Across all the layers
    D. Layers no longer form

Passage V

A chemistry student wishes to study weight relationships between compounds before and after they take part in reactions. Two experiments were conducted to investigate two different reactions. The reactions are shown below, together with the amount (grams) of each substance before and after each reaction has proceeded. Equations are balanced to show the number of each type of atom before and after the reactions.

Experiment 1					
	NaBr	+ AgNO$_3$	$\Rightarrow$	AgBr	+ NaNO$_3$
Initial Wt.	103	170		0	0
Final Wt.	0	0		188	85

Experiment 2						
	Na$_2$CO$_3$	+ 2HCl	$\Rightarrow$	2NaCl	+ H$_2$O (g)	+ CO$_2$
Initial Wt.	106	72		0	0	(?)
Final Wt.	0	0		117	18	(?)

(The student has measured the quantities he could, but was unable to weigh the CO$_2$ because it is a gas. Since it is a gas, he assumes it has negligible weight.)

28. In Experiment 1, the data indicate that after the reaction has proceeded:

    F. all of the Na originally present has been converted to Ag.
    G. there are fewer molecules of NaNO$_3$ than there were molecules of AgNO$_3$ at the outset.
    H. no NaBr remains.
    J. no AgBr remains.

29. Which of the following is (are) conserved in the reaction in Experiment 1?

    I. mass
    II. number of atoms
    III. amount of AgNO$_3$

    A. I only
    B. I and II only
    C. I and III only
    D. I, II, and III

30. In Experiment 2, the mass of the weighed products is:

    F. 0.
    G. less than the mass of reactants.
    H. equal to the mass of reactants.
    J. greater than the mass of reactants.

31. Experiment 2 differs from Experiment 1 in that:

    A. the number of atoms is not conserved.
    B. the reaction does not go to completion.
    C. there are no ionic compounds involved.
    D. gas is evolved.

32. Assuming the student is right in neglecting the weight of one of the products in Experiment 2, he can conclude from the data that:

    F. mass is consumed as the reaction proceeds.
    G. mass is produced as the reaction proceeds.
    H. energy is consumed as the reaction proceeds.
    J. mass is conserved as the reaction proceeds.

33. The student is advised of a means to weigh the CO$_2$ gas produced in the reaction, and finds this weight to be 43 grams. The student can now state that the two experiments:

    A. lead to similar conclusions: neither mass nor atoms are conserved.
    B. lead to similar conclusions: both mass and atoms are conserved.
    C. lead to different conclusions: the number of molecules is not the same for the reactants as for the products.
    D. lead to different conclusions: gases have negligible weight.

Passage VI

A series of three experiments was designed to investigate the interrelationships between various factors known to influence gases: temperature (Kelvin), pressure (atmospheres), volume (liters), and the number of moles of gas.

Experiment 1: A gas at 200 K and a volume of 0.30 liters was found to have a pressure of 0.40 atm. After the temperature was raised to 400 K while keeping the volume the same, the pressure was found to be 0.80 atm.

Experiment 2: A gas at 200 K had a pressure of 0.50 atm. when its volume was 1 liter. Its volume was then increased to 2 liters at constant temperature. The resulting pressure was 0.25 atm.

Experiment 3: Two moles of a gas were found to occupy 44.8 liters at 1 atm. pressure and 273 K. Four moles of the same gas are added to the system with temperature and pressure held constant, resulting in a new volume of 134.4 liters.

34. Which of the following hypotheses is (are) supported by the results of Experiment 1?

    I. The pressure of the gas is proportional to its volume at constant temperature.
    II. The volume of the gas is proportional to its temperature at constant pressure.
    III. The pressure of a gas is proportional to its temperature at constant volume.

    F. I only
    G. I and II only
    H. III only
    J. II and III only

35. The results of Experiment 2 support the hypothesis that if the temperature of a gas is held constant, then the pressure:

    A. increases as the volume increases.
    B. decreases as the volume increases.
    C. does not depend strongly on the volume.
    D. Cannot be determined from the given information

36. The result of Experiment 3 supports the hypothesis that if both the pressure and the temperature of a gas are held constant, then the volume:

    F. varies inversely with the number of moles of gas.
    G. varies directly with the number of moles of gas.
    H. is raised to a maximum value of 134.4 liters when additional gas is added.
    J. does not depend on the number of moles of gas.

37. An experimenter put 0.08 moles of gas into a 4-liter flask at 273 K and 0.448 atm. pressure. She allowed 0.02 moles of the gas to escape, and she put the remaining gas into a smaller flask that caused the pressure to remain at 0.448 atm. pressure, while the temperature was kept constant as well. According to Experiment 3, the volume of the smaller flask must be:

    A. 0.06 liter.
    B. 0.448 liters.
    C. 3 liters.
    D. Cannot be determined from the given information

38. Six moles of a gas originally at 0.1 atm. pressure and 273 K occupy a volume of 13.4 liters. The temperature is then changed to 300 K and the volume changed to 10.0 liters. To predict the final pressure on the six moles of gas, a student should use the results of:

    I. Experiment 1.
    II. Experiment 2.
    III. Experiment 3.

    F. I only
    G. II only
    H. I and II only
    J. I and III only

39. The final pressure of the gas described in the previous question will be:

    A. less than 0.1 atm. pressure.
    B. equal to 0.1 atm. pressure.
    C. greater than 0.1 atm pressure.
    D. Cannot be determined from the given information

NOTES AND STRATEGIES

Passage VII

To investigate the factors affecting the rate at which starch is broken down to sugar by the digestive enzyme salivary amylase, two experiments were performed. In both experiments, starch (in the form of a cracker) was mixed in a beaker with the enzyme, and the samples were removed every three minutes. Dipping special sugar indicators in the sample revealed the presence of starch in a sample (indicating that the cracker had not yet been completely digested).

Experiment 1: To test the effects of different pH levels on enzyme activity rate, one cracker and a standard amount of enzyme were placed in three beakers, each containing buffers of different pH. This procedure was repeated using standard amounts of water in place of the enzyme. All tests were carried out at optimal temperature. Starch and sugar levels (starch/sugar) from selected samples are shown in Table 1.

Table 1

CONTENTS OF BEAKERS	APPROXIMATE pH LEVELS	LEVELS OF STARCH/SUGAR			
		After 3 min.	*After 9 min.*	*After 15 min.*	*After 60 min.*
cracker + enzyme + buffer	5	high/none	high/none	high/low	moderate/moderate
	7	moderate/moderate	low/high	none/high	none/high
	9	high/none	high/none	high/low	moderate/moderate
cracker + water + buffer	5	high/none	high/none	high/none	high/none
	7	high/none	high/none	high/none	high/none
	9	high/none	high/none	high/none	high/none

Experiment 2: To test the effects of temperature on enzyme activity rate, one cracker and a standard amount of enzyme were placed in 3 beakers, each kept at different temperatures. This was also repeated using standard amounts of water in place of the enzyme. All tests were carried out at optimal pH. Starch and sugar levels (starch/sugar) from selected samples are shown in Table 2.

Table 2

CONTENTS OF BEAKERS	TEMPERATURES	LEVELS OF STARCH/SUGAR			
		After 3 min.	*After 9 min.*	*After 15 min.*	*After 60 min.*
cracker + enzyme	25° C	high/none	high/none	high/low	moderate/moderate
	37° C	moderate/moderate	low/high	none/high	none/high
	45° C	high/none	high/none	high/low	moderate/moderate
cracker + water	25° C	high/none	high/none	high/none	high/none
	37° C	high/none	high/none	high/none	high/none
	45° C	high/none	high/none	high/none	high/none

40. Under what conditions does salivary amylase appear to work best?

   F. Any pH level greater than 5 and any temperature greater than 25° C
   G. Any pH level greater than 5 and any temperature less than 45° C
   H. pH level of 9 and temperature equals 37° C
   J. pH level of 7 and temperature equals 37° C

41. The ingredient used as a control for both experiments is the:

   A. cracker.
   B. water.
   C. enzyme.
   D. starch/sugar level.

42. Which of the following hypotheses is supported by the results of Experiment 1?

    F. At the appropriate pH, water can break down starch, but at a slower rate than salivary amylase can.
    G. At any one-time interval, no differences in the effects of the three buffers on salivary amylase activity should be detectable.
    H. Salivary amylase can show activity at each of the three pH levels tested.
    J. The duration of time in which starch and enzyme remain in the beakers should have no effect on the amount of sugar produced.

43. Which of the following experimental designs would test the hypothesis that enzyme concentration can affect the rate of starch digestion?

    A. Using the same pH, temperature, and enzyme levels in all beakers, test additional samples at 90 minutes, 120 minutes, and 240 minutes.
    B. Using different pH, temperature, and enzyme levels in all beakers, test additional samples at 90 minutes, 120 minutes, and 240 minutes.
    C. Using the same pH and temperatures in all beakers, test additional samples with the enzyme at $\frac{1}{2} \cdot$ strength, $2 \cdot$ strength, and $4 \cdot$ strength.
    D. Using the same pH, temperature, and enzyme levels in all beakers, test additional samples after stirring for 3 minutes, 9 minutes, 15 minutes, and 60 minutes.

44. In Experiment 2, an additional beaker was tested at 70° C (cracker + enzyme). After 60 minutes, the sample showed high levels of starch and no sugar. Which of the following best explains this result?

    F. All the starch was destroyed at this high temperature.
    G. The enzyme does not work at all at this high temperature.
    H. Starch cannot be detected at this high temperature.
    J. Iodine and sugar indicators cannot function properly at this high temperature.

45. On the basis of the results of Experiment 1, what would probably occur if Experiment 2 were carried out at a pH level of 5?

    A. Digestion of starch to sugar would slowly begin in the beakers containing crackers plus water.
    B. Overall, digestion of starch to sugar would probably take place less efficiently.
    C. Overall, digestion of starch to sugar would probably take place more efficiently.
    D. Results would not change.

Passage VIII

Using electrical circuits, three experiments were performed to investigate the relationship between voltage (olts), resistance (ohms) (total resistance equals sum of individual resistances), and current (amperes.) Each experiment was set up with the following circuit design:

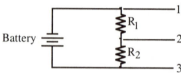

Experiment 1: Using a 6-volt battery (far left), and two 1,000-ohm resistors (R_1 and R_2), the measured voltages between points 1 and 2 and between points 2 and 3 were 3 volts each.

Experiment 2: When the battery voltage was increased to 12 volts, and the resistors were kept the same (1,000 ohms each), the measured voltages between points 1 and 2 and between points 2 and 3 were 6 volts each.

Experiment 3: Using the original 6-volt battery, R_1 was replaced with a 2,000-ohm resistor. The voltages measured between points 1 and 2 and between points 2 and 3 were 4 volts and 2 volts, respectively.

46. Judging from the results in Experiment 1 and Experiment 2, if the battery voltage were changed to 1.5 volts, what voltage would be expected between point 1 and point 2?

   F. 0.75 volts
   G. 1.5 volts
   H. 3.0 volts
   J. 6.0 volts

47. The experimenter studies the measurement made in the previous question, as well as those made earlier in Experiments 1, 2, and 3, and hypothesizes that:

   A. voltage measured across a resistor is inversely proportional to the value of that resistor.
   B. voltage measured across a resistor is directly proportional to the value of that resistor.
   C. voltage measured across a resistor is not related to the value of that resistor.
   D. voltage measured across a resistor equals the battery voltage.

48. When the experimenter recorded the current in the circuit of Experiment 1, it measured 0.003 amperes. In Experiment 3, however, the current measured 0.002 amperes. These results show that current and total resistances are:

   F. directly proportional.
   G. inversely proportional.
   H. equal.
   J. unrelated.

49. Which of the following formulas for the current in the circuit best summarizes the above results? (The battery voltage is given by V_b and the total resistance is given by R.)

   A. $V_b R$
   B. $\dfrac{R}{V_b}$
   C. $\dfrac{V_b}{R}$
   D. $V_b + R$

50. A new circuit is set up, similar in design to those in the experiments. The battery voltage and the size of the resistors are unknown, but the current measures 0.001 amperes. If the battery voltage is doubled and one of the two resistors is replaced with one having a smaller value, which answer most accurately describes the new current?

   F. It will be smaller than 0.001.
   G. It will be unchanged.
   H. It will be greater than 0.001.
   J. Cannot be determined from the given information

51. Which of the following single changes to Experiment 2 would produce a current of 0.004 amperes?

   A. Decrease the voltage to 8 volts.
   B. Increase the resistance to 3,000 ohms.
   C. Neither change will create a current of 0.004 amperes.
   D. Either change will create a current of 0.004 amperes.

NOTES AND STRATEGIES

Passage IX

Jean Baptiste Lamarck hypothesized the process of biological evolution before Charles Darwin was born. Some aspects of Lamarck's ideas and Darwin's ideas are presented below.

Lamarckism: Observations of the fossil record led Lamarck to believe that several lines of descent led to nature's broad diversity of organisms. Old fossils and recent fossils showed patterns leading to the characteristics of modern species. He believed that newer forms were more complex and more "perfectly" adapted to their environment. New adaptations could arise as the environment changed. Body organs that were used to cope with the environment became stronger and larger, while those not used deteriorated. For example, giraffes stretching their necks to reach higher leaves would develop longer necks. In addition, such changes in structure could then be passed on to offspring (these acquired characteristics could be inherited).

Darwinism: Based on the fossil and geologic record, Darwin also came to believe that various modern species were related through descent from common ancestors. He also noted that the great diversity of organisms that he observed during his travels were all very well adapted to their environments. The adaptations, however, did not come about through "coping" or usage. Instead, individuals from a population can each show slight genetic or "heritable" differences (variability) in a trait. If such differences, by chance alone, give the individual some reproductive advantage (he or she can successfully produce more offspring than other members of the population), then more individuals with that trait will make up the next generation. Through this "natural selection" of individuals with characteristics that give them a slight advantage in their particular environment, species appear to become very well suited to their natural world. However, "perfection" is not a useful term since the environment is constantly changing. The adaptations that are advantageous "today" may not be advantageous "tomorrow" under different conditions.

52. A major difference between Lamarck and Darwin relates to their views on:

    F. the diversity of organisms in the natural world.
    G. the significance of fossils.
    H. the importance of adaptations to the environment.
    J. the way adaptations come about.

53. Which viewpoint supports the idea that present-day species are descended from earlier forms?

    A. Lamarckism
    B. Darwinism
    C. Both viewpoints
    D. Neither viewpoint

54. Which statement might be used by a Darwinist to explain the extinction of a species?

    F. The environment changed, and not enough individuals had traits or adaptations well suited to the new conditions.
    G. The environment changed, and body parts could not be manipulated enough to adapt to new conditions.
    H. As the environment changed, the individuals present were not "perfect" enough.
    J. As the environment changed, there was no "natural selection."

55. Darwin might dispute the Lamarckian idea of inheriting acquired characteristics by pointing out that:

    A. giraffes with short necks may do just as well as those with long necks.
    B. giraffes that break a leg and walk around on three legs all their lives still do not produce three-legged offspring.
    C. giraffes had shorter necks millions of years ago.
    D. giraffes that break a leg would not be able to reach the highest leaves.

56. Many species of moles live underground, in the dark. These species often have small, almost dysfunctional eyes. Which of the following statement(s) would a Lamarckian thinker use to explain this phenomenon?

    I. Moles without eyesight are better adapted for survival underground and therefore produce more offspring.
    II. Disuse of eyes in the dark led to their deterioration in mole species.
    III. Eye deterioration can be transferred to a mole's genes, which are then passed on to the next generation.

    F. I only
    G. II only
    H. II and III only
    J. I, II, and III

57. Which factor is vital to Darwin's ideas, but not to those of Lamarck?

    A. The fossil record
    B. An examination of modern species
    C. The inheritance of adaptations
    D. Chance

58. A few individuals in a population have an adaptation that enables them to tolerate extremely cold temperatures. In their lifetimes, the environment never reaches such extremes. If all other traits are the same among individuals, what would a Darwinist predict about the number of offspring left in the next generation by these individuals, compared to the number left by other members of the population?

    F. These individuals will leave approximately the same number of offspring.
    G. These individuals will leave more offspring.
    H. These individuals will leave fewer offspring.
    J. These individuals will probably not leave any offspring.

Passage X

How did life originate on the planet Earth? Two opposing views are presented.

Scientist 1: The idea that Earth could have given rise to life independently is mistaken. Life on this planet must have come from elsewhere for several reasons. First of all, complex life appears very suddenly in the geological record. Secondly, all life on Earth has a very similar biochemistry. If life originated on Earth, one would expect regional variations in biochemistry, similar to the variations in species spread over large areas. Finally, the time when life first appeared in the geological record was also a time when large numbers of meteorites struck the Earth. The meteorites must have caused life to appear on the Earth. The simplest hypothesis is that the meteorites brought life with them.

Scientist 2: Life need not have been imported from outer space. The chemicals required for life existed on the surface of the Earth at the time life first appeared. The fact that all life has a similar biochemistry can be explained by considering that any group of chemicals that won the race to life would probably have used the "almost-living" as food. Since we can offer explanations for what happened without relying on a meteorite of unknown composition that might have fallen to Earth, we should stick to hypotheses that have fewer unknowns.

59. Which of the following is an assumption of Scientist 1?

    A. Complex life forms can develop quickly.
    B. Meteorites burn up as soon as they hit the Earth's atmosphere.
    C. There is a cause-and-effect relationship between meteors falling and the origin of life.
    D. The changes on the Earth's surface due to the presence of life attracted meteor showers.

60. Which of the following, if true, strengthens Scientist 2's argument the most?

    F. Only 5% more meteors than normal fell on the Earth during the time life began.
    G. Only 5% of the meteorites studied contained organic molecules.
    H. A simulation of early Earth chemistry showed the spontaneous formation of complex biomolecules.
    J. Meteorites containing amoebas have been found.

61. Which of the following, if true, strengthens Scientist 1's argument the most?

    A. Only 5% more meteors than normal fell on the Earth during the time life began.
    B. Only 5% of the meteorites studied contained organic molecules.
    C. A simulation of early Earth chemistry showed the spontaneous formation of complex biomolecules.
    D. Meteorites containing amoebas have been found.

62. With which explanation of the similar biochemistry of all life on Earth would Scientist 1 most likely agree?

    F. A single chemical pathway to life exists.
    G. Life arose from a single source.
    H. Life is not varied.
    J. Meteors are simple.

63. With which explanation of the similar biochemistry of all life on Earth would Scientist 2 most likely agree?

    A. A single chemical pathway to life exists.
    B. Life arose from a single source.
    C. Life is not varied.
    D. Meteors are simple.

64. Which scientist would be likely to disagree with the idea that life on different planets could have different biochemistries?

    F. Scientist 1
    G. Scientist 2
    H. Both scientists
    J. Neither scientist

65. Which of the following questions would be the most difficult for Scientist 1 to defend his theory against?

    A. Why was there more meteorite activity earlier in Earth's history?
    B. Why have other meteors not brought other life based on a different biochemistry?
    C. Why did complex life emerge suddenly?
    D. Why should meteor activity have any connection to the origin of life?

66. Could Scientist 2 believe that life exists on other planets without affecting his hypothesis?

   F. Yes, as long as he believes that life elsewhere has a different biochemistry.
   G. Yes, because wherever the chemicals required for life exist, life can begin.
   H. No, because then he has to admit that meteorites brought life from these planets.
   J. No, because then he has to admit that meteorites that came from pieces of similar planets brought life to the Earth.

Passage XI

What will the end of the universe be like? Two opposing views are presented.

Scientist 1: The universe will die out with a whimper because the energy of the big bang that created the universe will spread itself out over larger and larger regions of space. Since there is only so much energy in the universe, every cubic foot must hold, on the average, less energy as time goes on. In the end everything will get so cold that all motion will stop. That will be the true end of time.

Scientist 2: The idea that the universe will spread itself too thin and freeze is seriously flawed. Such theories do not take into account the gravitational attractions of the bits of matter in the universe for each other. Gravity can act as a cosmic glue to keep the universe from dissolving into nothingness.

67. Which of the following is a major assumption of Scientist 1?

   A. All matter consists of atoms.
   B. There is a limited amount of energy in the universe.
   C. Gravity does not exist in interstellar space.
   D. The universe is contracting.

68. Which of the following facts, if true, does not help Scientist 2's hypothesis?

   F. It is shown that the galaxies are moving away from each other with a constant speed.
   G. It is shown that the galaxies are moving towards each other with a constant speed.
   H. It is shown that the galaxies are moving towards each other with a constant acceleration.
   J. It is shown that the galaxies are not moving at all relative to each other.

69. It has been calculated that if the universe has a mass greater than or equal to m, then the universe will eventually collapse on itself. Scientist 1 would likely say that the mass of the universe:

   A. is equal to m.
   B. is less than or equal to m.
   C. is greater than m.
   D. is less than m.

70. If Scientist 2 claims that the universe is contracting, what would he expect the average temperature of the universe to be in ten billion years?

   F. Higher than now
   G. Lower than now
   H. Same as now
   J. No comparison is possible

71. What must be true about the energy content of the universe if Scientist 1 is correct?

   A. It is increasing.
   B. It is decreasing.
   C. It is a constant.
   D. It increased at the moment of the big bang, and decreased afterwards.

72. What would happen if the forces moving the galaxies farther out were exactly balanced by the forces pulling them together?

   F. The galaxies would stop moving.
   G. The galaxies would move in a straight line with constant speed.
   H. The galaxies would move in a straight line with constant acceleration.
   J. The galaxies would move back and forth in a straight line.

STEP THREE

Passage XII

How old is the Earth? Two opposing views are presented.

Scientist 1: The Earth is approximately five billion years old. We know this to be true because of radioactive dating. Some chemical elements are unstable and will fall apart into smaller pieces over time. This disintegration occurs over a period of time that is very regular for the particular element. In general, we talk about the half-life of the element, which is the time necessary for one-half of the material to disintegrate. This time is constant whether we have an ounce or a ton of the material. So, by measuring the relative amounts of the material left and the disintegration products, we can form an accurate idea of how old the Earth is by determining how many half-lives have occurred.

Scientist 2: The argument that supports the hypothesis that the Earth is only five billion years old is seriously flawed. What the argument fails to take into account is that the Earth is the constant recipient of a shower of cosmic debris in the form of meteorites. These meteorites replenish the stock of radioactive material on the surface of the Earth, making it seem as though the Earth has gone through fewer half-lives than it really has. Therefore, all estimates of the age of the Earth based on radioactive dating are too low.

73. Which of the following is a major assumption of Scientist 1?

    A. The Earth has life that recycles carbon-14.
    B. The Earth is five billion years old.
    C. The radioactive material was formed at the same time as the Earth.
    D. There is no longer any radioactivity on the Earth.

74. Which of the following is a major assumption of Scientist 2?

    F. The meteorites that land on the Earth are radioactive.
    G. Few meteorites have landed on the Earth.
    H. The Earth is more than five billion years old.
    J. The Earth is highly radioactive.

75. Which of the following, if true, would best refute Scientist 2's argument?

    A. Recent meteorites have been found to be radioactive.
    B. The Earth has a greater amount of radioactive material on the surface than in the mantle.
    C. The Earth's orbit intersects the orbits of a number of meteorites.
    D. Few meteorites have been found to contain radioactive material.

76. Which of the following would be most likely if Scientist 2's hypothesis were correct?

    F. The amount of radioactive material and its disintegration products on the Earth has decreased over time.
    G. The amount of radioactive material and its disintegration products has increased over time.
    H. The amount of radioactive material and its disintegration products has stayed essentially the same over time.
    J. The Earth will reach a critical mass and explode.

77. Which of the following would be most likely if Scientist 1's hypothesis were correct?

    A. The amount of radioactive material and its disintegration products has decreased over time.
    B. The amount of radioactive material and its disintegration products has increased over time.
    C. The amount of radioactive material and its disintegration products has stayed essentially the same over time.
    D. The Earth will reach a critical mass and explode.

78. Which of the following conditions, if true, would prevent an estimation of the Earth's age by Scientist 1's method?

    F. No radioactive disintegration has occurred.
    G. Only some of the radioactive material has disintegrated.
    H. Eighty percent of the radioactive material has disintegrated.
    J. All of the radioactive material has disintegrated.

NOTES AND STRATEGIES

STEP THREE

SECTION THREE—SCIENCE REASONING QUIZZES

DIRECTIONS: This section contains three Science Reasoning quizzes. Complete each quiz while being timed. Each passage is followed by several questions. After reading a passage, choose the best answer to each question. You may refer to the passages as often as necessary. You are NOT permitted to use a calculator. Answers are on page 207.

QUIZ I (10 questions; 9 minutes)

Passage I

The ecological pyramid below shows the relative biomass[†] of organisms at each trophic feeding level of a marine food chain.

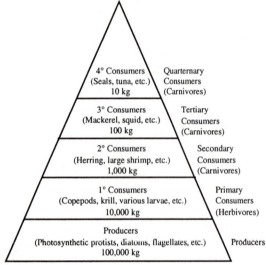

[†] *Biomass:* Total dry weight of organisms (usable chemical energy stored in organic matter) at each trophic level at any given time.

1. According to the diagram, the trophic level with the largest relative biomass is the:

   A. 4° consumers.
   B. 3° and 2° consumers.
   C. 1° consumers.
   D. producers.

2. From the information in the diagram, one can conclude that at any given time:

   F. 10 seals may be found for every mackerel.
   G. the relative dry weight of all carnivores combined is far greater than that of the herbivores alone.
   H. only 1% of all producers live long enough to be eaten by a mackerel.
   J. the relative dry weight of every consumer trophic level is usually less than that of the trophic level on which they feed.

3. Organisms from which trophic level are most likely to be found near the water surface where light can penetrate?

   A. 4° consumers
   B. 2° consumers
   C. 3° consumers
   D. producers

4. If there were an additional trophic level of carnivores (5° consumers), its relative biomass at any given time would be approximately:

   F.   11 kg.
   G. 1,000,000 kg.
   H.   1 kg.
   J.   111 kg.

5. The best explanation for biomass being measured as dry weight is:

   A. if water weight were included, efficiency ratios at each trophic level would be unpredictable.
   B. body fluids contribute little to the mass of marine organisms.
   C. water molecules contain little or no usable chemical energy.
   D. each trophic level contains a different amount of water.

Passage II

The table below shows various characteristics of different layers of the atmosphere.

Approximate Altitude (km)	Layers of the Atmosphere	Approximate Mean Temperature (° C)	Clouds
60,000			
6,000			
	THERMOSPHERE		
600		1200	
80		−90	
	MESOSPHERE		
50		−3	
	STRATOSPHERE		Cirrus
12		−50	
			Cirrostratus
5	TROPOSPHERE		Altostratus
0		18	Nimbostratus

6. Which statement accurately describes the relationship between the approximate altitude and the approximate mean temperature of the layers of the atmosphere?

   F. As altitude increases, temperature increases.
   G. As altitude increases, temperature decreases.
   H. As altitude increases, temperature first decreases then continuously increases.
   J. As altitude increases, temperature first decreases, then increases, then decreases, and then increases.

7. Based on the information in the table, the atmospheric layer with the narrowest range of altitude is the:

   A. thermosphere.
   B. troposphere.
   C. mesosphere.
   D. stratosphere.

8. The type of cloud(s) most likely to consist of ice crystals is (are):

   F. nimbostratus only.
   G. nimbostratus and altostratus.
   H. cirrus and cirrostratus.
   J. cirrostratus only.

9. The absorption of solar heat energy increases as the gases of the atmosphere become rarefied. The layer of the atmosphere that appears most rarefied is the:

   A. thermosphere.
   B. mesosphere.
   C. stratosphere.
   D. troposphere.

10. According to the table, which atmospheric layer shows a decrease in temperature of approximately 3° C for every 1-kilometer increase in altitude?

    F. thermosphere
    G. mesosphere
    H. stratosphere
    J. troposphere

STEP THREE

QUIZ II (10 questions; 9 minutes)

Passage I

The chart below shows in outline form a common means of analyzing a sample solution for various cations (positive ions). Ions above the horizontal arrows are those that are suspected to be present in the sample solution; the substances in the boxes are the reagents added as tests (0.3 M H^+ is acidic, NH_4OH is alkaline); the products shown next to the arrows pointing downward are solid precipitates resulting from the tests. Tests for specific ions need not always start from the beginning of the sequence.

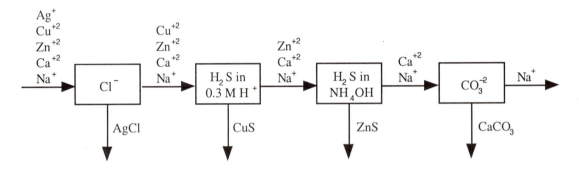

1. According to the chart, which precipitate indicates if silver (Ag) is present in the sample?

   A. AgCl
   B. Ag
   C. CuS
   D. ZnS

2. If a solution containing silver (Ag) nitrate and cupric (Cu) nitrate is tested according to this scheme, an experimenter will:

   F. first observe AgCl on treatment with Cl^-, and next observe CuS on treatment with H_2S.
   G. first observe CuS on treatment with Cl^-, and next observe AgCl on treatment with H_2S.
   H. first observe $CaCO_3$ on treatment with CO_3^{-2}, and next observe AgCl on treatment with Cl^-.
   J. observe no reactions, since the scheme does not test for nitrate.

3. What is the minimum number of tests necessary to confirm the composition of an unknown solution that contains no other positive ions except Cu^{+2} or Zn^{+2}, but not both?

   A. 1
   B. 2
   C. 3
   D. 4

4. Which statement is most correct concerning the separation of Cu^{+2} from Zn^{+2} in the same solution?

   F. Completely different test reagents are used in each of the two steps.
   G. The same test reagents are used in each of the two steps.
   H. The same test reagents are used, but the first step must be in an alkaline environment while the second step must be in an acidic environment.
   J. The same test reagents are used, but the first step must be in an acidic environment while the second step must be in an alkaline environment.

5. A clear solution is found, by a method not discussed here, to contain chloride ion (Cl^-). From the information given here, what ion could not be present in the solution?

   A. Carbonate (CO^{-2})
   B. Cupric (Cu^{+2})
   C. Silver (Ag^+)
   D. Zinc (Zn^{+2})

Passage II

The chart below shows the flavor preferences of white-tailed deer when offered various fluids to drink at different ages.

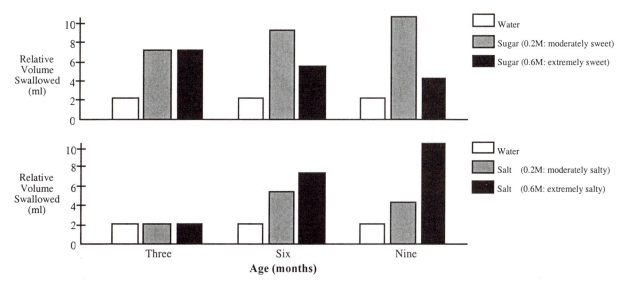

6. Which category on the chart shows no preference between water and the experimental flavor?

   F. Three months of age/sugar
   G. Six months of age/salt
   H. Three months of age/salt
   J. Nine months of age/sugar

7. Which statement about white-tailed deer is supported by the information in the chart?

   A. As age increases, the preference for all tested sugars increases.
   B. As age increases, the preference for all tested salts increases.
   C. As age increases, differences between sugars cannot be detected, and differences between salts cannot be detected.
   D. As age increases, differences between sugars can be detected, and differences between salts can be detected.

8. The flavor preference that fluctuates most irregularly with age is:

   F. moderately salty.
   G. moderately sweet.
   H. extremely salty.
   J. extremely sweet.

9. Based on the trends shown in the chart, which of the following predictions is most reasonable for one-year-old white-tailed deer?

   A. Moderately sweet and moderately salty will be most preferred.
   B. Extremely sweet and extremely salty will be most preferred.
   C. Moderately sweet and extremely salty will be most preferred.
   D. Extremely sweet and moderately salty will be most preferred.

10. Which of the following conclusions about water is NOT consistent with the data in the chart?

    F. Water is never preferred over any tested flavors.
    G. Before the age of six months, white-tailed deer cannot taste the difference between water and sugar or between water and salt.
    H. At the age of three months, both salty fluids are equal to the water swallowed.
    J. As age increases, the volume of water swallowed remains the same.

 STEP THREE

QUIZ III (11 questions; 9 minutes)

Passage I

The table below shows the first three ionization energies for the atoms hydrogen through potassium. The first ionization energy, E_1, is the energy (in kilocalories per mole of atoms) that must be added in order to remove the first electron. E_2 is the energy required to remove a second electron once the first has been removed, and E_3 is the energy needed to remove a third electron. If an atom lacks a second or third electron, no value is given in the table.

IONIZATION ENERGIES OF THE ELEMENTS (kcal/mole)				
Atomic No.	Element	E_1	E_2	E_3
1	H	313.6	-	-
2	He	566.8	1254	-
3	Li	124.3	1744	2823
4	Be	214.9	419.9	3548
5	B	191.3	580.0	874.5
6	C	259.6	562.2	1104
7	N	335.1	682.8	1094
8	O	314.0	810.6	1267
9	F	401.8	806.7	1445
10	Ne	497.2	947.2	1500
11	Na	118.5	1091	1652
12	Mg	176.3	346.6	1848
13	Al	138.0	434.1	655.9
14	Si	187.9	376.8	771.7
15	P	241.8	453.2	695.5
16	S	238.9	540	807
17	Cl	300.0	548.9	920.2
18	Ar	363.4	637	943.3
19	K	100.1	733.6	1100

1. For a given element, the ionization energies increase in the order:

   A. E_3, E_2, E_1.
   B. E_2, E_1, E_3.
   C. E_1, E_2, E_3.
   D. Order varies.

2. A student suspects that there may be an atom for which the second ionization energy is roughly twice that of the first, and the third is roughly twice that of the second. Which of the following atoms best fits this relationship?

   F. Be
   G. C
   H. Ne
   J. Ar

3. As atomic number increases, the trend in the values of E_2 is:

   A. generally upward.
   B. generally downward.
   C. upward for a few values, then suddenly downward, followed by another increase, *etc*.
   D. downward for a few values, then suddenly upward, followed by a decrease again, *etc*.

4. If the chart were continued to the element having atomic number 20, its value for E_1 would be expected to be closest to:

   F. 20.
   G. 90.
   H. 140.
   J. 730.

5. An experimenter has at her disposal a means of providing an atom with any energy up to 200 kcal/mole. From how many different atoms could she remove one electron?

   A. 7
   B. 8
   C. 11
   D. 12

Passage II

A physics student performed two sets of experiments designed to examine the factors that influence the motion of falling objects.

Experiment 1: A stone was dropped from a steep cliff while a camera, mounted on a tripod on the ground, took photographs at 1-second intervals. Back in the laboratory, the same procedure was repeated in the absence (nearly) of air inside a huge vacuum chamber.

Experiment 2: The experiments were repeated (on the cliff and inside the vacuum chamber) using a stone and a cork with identical masses dropped at the same time. At the cliff, the stone hit the ground first. In the vacuum chamber, both objects hit the ground together.

6. Assuming that air acts to resist the downward acceleration of the stone, how will the total time required to reach the ground in the vacuum chamber compare to the time required to reach the ground from the cliff?

   F. Longer time in air than in vacuum chamber
   G. Longer time in vacuum chamber than in air
   H. Same time in each
   J. Cannot be determined from the given information

7. If part of Experiment 1 were repeated on the moon, where the pull of gravity is one sixth that of the Earth, the stone's downward speed would increase as it falls (*i.e.*, it would accelerate) but the rate of increase in speed would only be one sixth as great as on the Earth. When the photos taken at 1-second intervals on the moon are compared to the photos taken on Earth, the series of moon pictures of the stone will be:

   A. closer together.
   B. farther apart.
   C. identical.
   D. closer at some times and farther apart at others.

8. In Experiment 2, the observed results can be explained by the hypothesis that:

   F. heavier objects fall more rapidly than lighter ones.
   G. a cork of the same mass as a stone is smaller than the stone, and it encounters more air resistance.
   H. a cork of the same mass as a stone is larger than the stone, and it encounters more air resistance.
   J. the gravitational acceleration of objects toward the ground diminishes when air is not present.

9. In Experiment 1, gravity accelerates the stone as it falls from the cliff, causing it to pick up speed as it drops. Which of the following series of pictures most resembles how the stone appears as it drops?

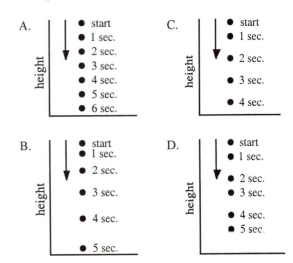

10. The experimenter devises a means of suspending the Earth's gravity for short periods of time. Armed with this technique, he drops the stone (on Earth, in air, under conditions of normal gravity), and then suspends gravity 2 seconds after the stone has been falling and leaves it off for the next minute. Recalling that gravity causes the stone's downward speed to increase continually, choose the "photo" that best illustrates, in 1-second intervals, this experiment.

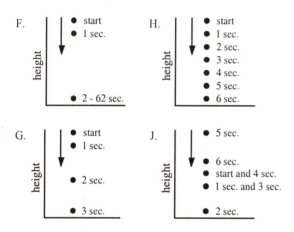

11. If Experiment 2 were repeated on the airless moon, which prediction would be correct?

    A. The cork would fall more slowly than on the Earth.
    B. The cork would fall as rapidly as the stone.
    C. Both predictions are correct.
    D. Neither prediction is correct.

 STEP THREE

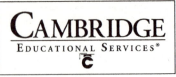

AMERICA'S #1 STANDARDS-BASED SCHOOL IMPROVEMENT

Strategy Summary Sheet
ACT • PLAN • EXPLORE—SCIENCE REASONING

STRUCTURE OF THE ACT, PLAN, AND EXPLORE SCIENCE REASONING TESTS: The ACT Science Reasoning Test is 35 minutes long with 40 multiple-choice questions. (The PLAN is 30 items in 25 minutes; the EXPLORE is 28 items in 30 minutes). There will be about seven reading passages divided among biology, Earth/space sciences, chemistry, and physics. While there is no general ladder of difficulty (increasing difficulty with increasing problem number), the questions within a question group tend to get harder towards the end of the group of questions. There will be six to eight groups with five to seven questions each, preceded by a scientific discussion. The approximate distribution of the Science Reasoning problems is as follows:

	ACT (40 questions)	PLAN (30 questions)	EXPLORE (28 questions)
Data Representation Passages	15	17	12
Research Summary Passages	18	6	10
Conflicting Viewpoints Passages	7	7	6

SCIENCE REASONING GENERAL STRATEGIES: This section tests your reasoning skills, not your scientific knowledge. Most of the passages have all of the information you will need to answer the questions. In some cases, background information at the level of your high school general science courses is required, but do not assume data that is not given. The following are basic general Science Reasoning strategies:

- *Pacing is important.* Remember that within the 35-minute limit, you will have to read and think about seven reading passages and the accompanying question sets. In other words, you will have an average of just five minutes per passage. You will need to work quickly to answer every question.

- Before reading any passage, quickly *glance over each passage and code each according to the type of passage* in order to determine the order in which you will attack the passages. Identifying and coding each passage should take no more than five seconds.

- *Do not preview the question stems.* Previewing the Science Reasoning question stems will only confuse you and slow you down, since they tend to be confusing without having first read the passage.

- It is important to only *read the passage thoroughly once,* rather than skimming it several times. The material can be difficult to understand, thus it is important to read thoughtfully and carefully. *Be an active reader.* Use your pencil to underline key words and points of information. That way, you will be able to locate them easily when answering the questions.

- When a reading passage includes tables or graphs, make sure you *read and understand the labels* on axes, columns, and rows. You need to know what information is being presented and what units of measure are being used.

- Tables and graphs present results, often of observations or experiments. Questions will usually ask you to spot patterns in the data, so *look for trends* such as upward movement, downward movement, inverse variation, and the like.

SCIENCE

- Many passages will contain much more information than you need to answer a particular question. In your search for a logical conclusion, *do not be misled by data that do not relate to the question at hand.*

- The experiments described in Research Summary questions are based on scientific assumptions. However, if an assumption is faulty, the experiment may not prove what it claims to prove, and conclusions drawn from it may be invalid. Therefore, for questions that ask about the validity of a scientific conclusion, *consider the validity of underlying assumptions.*

- The arguments presented in Conflicting Viewpoint questions are also based on scientific assumptions. Again, *if the assumption is wrong, the entire argument is open to challenge.* Assumptions that are based on scientific fact add strength to an argument; faulty assumptions weaken it.

- Offering the assumptions that you started with as proof of your argument is called circular reasoning, and this is not acceptable proof. For that reason, any conclusions discussed in Science Reasoning passages or offered as answer choices must be based on additional evidence (*e.g.*, experiments) to be valid. *Beware of any conclusions that are nothing more than a restatement of an underlying premise.*

- All the information you need to answer the questions is provided in the passage—do not imply any information not given or relate previous experience to the passage. *Pay attention to material noted with an asterisk.*

- *Transcribe your answers from the test booklet to the answer sheet in groups* (by passage). However, when you get to the last passage, transcribe each answer as it is determined.

STRATEGIES FOR EACH TYPE OF PASSAGE:

1. *Data Representation*: When given data in the form of a graph or a chart, pay particular attention to the scale, units, legend, and other noted information.

2. *Research Summary*: When given multiple experiments, identify the controls and variables. Note that the controls must remain the same and that variables can only change one at a time in all experiments.

3. *Conflicting Viewpoints*: When given two points of view on a topic, identify the main points of difference and the logical value of each argument. After you understand the nature of the passage, attack the questions.

STRATEGIES FOR EACH TYPE OF QUESTION:

1. *Comprehension*: Recognize basic concepts. Read carefully. Make sure your answers consider appropriate scales and units. Also, note the difference between absolute and percentage changes.

2. *Analysis*: Identify relationships and trends. Pay particular attention to direct and inverse relationships.

3. *Application*: Draw conclusions, predict outcomes, and synthesize new information. In answering application questions, beware of "all, none, always, never." Remember that a single case of contradictory evidence is all that is necessary to disprove an absolute theory.

ADDITIONAL NOTES AND STRATEGIES FROM IN-CLASS DISCUSSION: _____

_____

_____

_____

STEP FOUR: PRACTICE TEST REINFORCEMENT

ACT • PLAN • EXPLORE SCIENCE REASONING

STEP FOUR: PRACTICE TEST REINFORCEMENT

CAMBRIDGE COURSE CONCEPT OUTLINE

AMERICA'S #1 STANDARDS-BASED SCHOOL IMPROVEMENT

Cambridge Course Concept Outline
STEP FOUR

I. **ACT SCIENCE REASONING STEP FOUR PROGRESS REPORTS** (p. 111)

    A. ACT • PLAN EXPLORE SCIENCE REASONING STEP FOUR STUDENT PROGRESS REPORT (p. 111)

    B. ACT • PLAN EXPLORE SCIENCE REASONING STEP FOUR INSTRUCTOR PROGRESS REPORT (p. 113)

II. **ACT SCIENCE REASONING PRACTICE TEST BUBBLE SHEETS** (p. 115)

III. **ACT SCIENCE REASONING PRACTICE TEST I** (p. 125)

IV. **ACT SCIENCE REASONING PRACTICE TEST II** (p. 135)

V. **ACT SCIENCE REASONING PRACTICE TEST III** (p. 145)

VI. **ACT SCIENCE REASONING PRACTICE TEST IV** (p. 157)

ACT SCIENCE REASONING
STEP FOUR PROGRESS REPORT
(Student Copy)

DIRECTIONS: These progress reports are designed to help you monitor your ACT Science Reasoning Practice Test progress. Complete the assigned problems, correct your answers, and record both the number and percentage of problems that you answered correctly. Identify the date on which you completed each section of the tests. List the numbers of any problems that you would like your instructor to review in class.

Transfer this information to the Instructor Copy, and then give that report to your instructor.

Name _____ Student ID _____ Date _____

ACT SCIENCE REASONING PRACTICE TESTS
(Student Copy)

ACT Science Reasoning Practice Test	Total # Possible	Assigned	# Correct	% Correct	Date Completed	Problem #s to Review
1. Practice Test I (p. 125)	40					
2. Practice Test II (p. 135)	40					
3. Practice Test III (p. 145)	40					
4. Practice Test IV (p. 157)	40					

PROGRESS REPORTS

ACT SCIENCE REASONING
STEP FOUR PROGRESS REPORT
(Instructor Copy)

DIRECTIONS: Transfer the information from your Student Copy to the Instructor Copy below. Leave the last three bolded columns blank. Your instructor will use them to evaluate your progress. When finished, give these reports to your instructor.

Name _____ Student ID _____ Date _____

ACT SCIENCE REASONING PRACTICE TESTS
(Instructor Copy)

	Total #						Instructor Skill Evaluation (Check One Per Exercise)		
Exercise	Possible	Assigned	# Correct	% Correct	Date Completed	Problem #s to Review	**Mastered**	**Partially Mastered**	**Not Mastered**
1. Practice Test I (p. 125)	40								
2. Practice Test II (p. 135)	40								
3. Practice Test III (p. 145)	40								
4. Practice Test IV (p. 157)	40								

ACT Practice Test I Bubble Sheet

Name ____________________ Student ID Number ____________________

Date ____________________ Instructor ____________________ Course/Session Number ____________________

TEST 1—ENGLISH

1 A B C D	16 F G H J	31 A B C D	46 F G H J	61 A B C D
2 F G H J	17 A B C D	32 F G H J	47 A B C D	62 F G H J
3 A B C D	18 F G H J	33 A B C D	48 F G H J	63 A B C D
4 F G H J	19 A B C D	34 F G H J	49 A B C D	64 F G H J
5 A B C D	20 F G H J	35 A B C D	50 F G H J	65 A B C D
6 F G H J	21 A B C D	36 F G H J	51 A B C D	66 F G H J
7 A B C D	22 F G H J	37 A B C D	52 F G H J	67 A B C D
8 F G H J	23 A B C D	38 F G H J	53 A B C D	68 F G H J
9 A B C D	24 F G H J	39 A B C D	54 F G H J	69 A B C D
10 F G H J	25 A B C D	40 F G H J	55 A B C D	70 F G H J
11 A B C D	26 F G H J	41 A B C D	56 F G H J	71 A B C D
12 F G H J	27 A B C D	42 F G H J	57 A B C D	72 F G H J
13 A B C D	28 F G H J	43 A B C D	58 F G H J	73 A B C D
14 F G H J	29 A B C D	44 F G H J	59 A B C D	74 F G H J
15 A B C D	30 F G H J	45 A B C D	60 F G H J	75 A B C D

TEST 2—MATHEMATICS

1 A B C D E	13 A B C D E	25 A B C D E	37 A B C D E	49 A B C D E
2 F G H J K	14 F G H J K	26 F G H J K	38 F G H J K	50 F G H J K
3 A B C D E	15 A B C D E	27 A B C D E	39 A B C D E	51 A B C D E
4 F G H J K	16 F G H J K	28 F G H J K	40 F G H J K	52 F G H J K
5 A B C D E	17 A B C D E	29 A B C D E	41 A B C D E	53 A B C D E
6 F G H J K	18 F G H J K	30 F G H J K	42 F G H J K	54 F G H J K
7 A B C D E	19 A B C D E	31 A B C D E	43 A B C D E	55 A B C D E
8 F G H J K	20 F G H J K	32 F G H J K	44 F G H J K	56 F G H J K
9 A B C D E	21 A B C D E	33 A B C D E	45 A B C D E	57 A B C D E
10 F G H J K	22 F G H J K	34 F G H J K	46 F G H J K	58 F G H J K
11 A B C D E	23 A B C D E	35 A B C D E	47 A B C D E	59 A B C D E
12 F G H J K	24 F G H J K	36 F G H J K	48 F G H J K	60 F G H J K

TEST 3—READING

1 A B C D	9 A B C D	17 A B C D	25 A B C D	33 A B C D
2 F G H J	10 F G H J	18 F G H J	26 F G H J	34 F G H J
3 A B C D	11 A B C D	19 A B C D	27 A B C D	35 A B C D
4 F G H J	12 F G H J	20 F G H J	28 F G H J	36 F G H J
5 A B C D	13 A B C D	21 A B C D	29 A B C D	37 A B C D
6 F G H J	14 F G H J	22 F G H J	30 F G H J	38 F G H J
7 A B C D	15 A B C D	23 A B C D	31 A B C D	39 A B C D
8 F G H J	16 F G H J	24 F G H J	32 F G H J	40 F G H J

TEST 4—SCIENCE REASONING

1 A B C D	9 A B C D	17 A B C D	25 A B C D	33 A B C D
2 F G H J	10 F G H J	18 F G H J	26 F G H J	34 F G H J
3 A B C D	11 A B C D	19 A B C D	27 A B C D	35 A B C D
4 F G H J	12 F G H J	20 F G H J	28 F G H J	36 F G H J
5 A B C D	13 A B C D	21 A B C D	29 A B C D	37 A B C D
6 F G H J	14 F G H J	22 F G H J	30 F G H J	38 F G H J
7 A B C D	15 A B C D	23 A B C D	31 A B C D	39 A B C D
8 F G H J	16 F G H J	24 F G H J	32 F G H J	40 F G H J

ACT Practice Test II Bubble Sheet

Name _____ Student ID Number _____

Date _____ Instructor _____ Course/Session Number _____

TEST 1—ENGLISH

(Answer bubbles 1–75, options A/B/C/D or F/G/H/J)

TEST 2—MATHEMATICS

(Answer bubbles 1–60, options A/B/C/D/E or F/G/H/J/K)

TEST 3—READING

(Answer bubbles 1–40, options A/B/C/D or F/G/H/J)

TEST 4—SCIENCE REASONING

(Answer bubbles 1–40, options A/B/C/D or F/G/H/J)

Photocopying not allowed without Cambridge licensing agreement.

ACT Practice Test III Bubble Sheet

ACT Practice Test IV Bubble Sheet

ACT • PLAN • EXPLORE
SCIENCE REASONING

ACT SCIENCE REASONING
PRACTICE TEST I

SCIENCE REASONING
35 Minutes—40 Questions

DIRECTIONS: There are seven passages in this test. Each passage is followed by several questions. After reading a passage, choose the best answer to each question and fill in the corresponding oval on your answer document. You may refer to the passages as often as necessary. You are NOT permitted to use a calculator on this test. Answers are on page 208.

Passage I

The chart below shows several physical properties of compounds called alkanes, which are long "chains" of carbons to which hydrogen atoms are attached. As an example, the compound propane, which has three carbons, has the structural formula:

$$CH_3—CH_2—CH_3$$

PHYSICAL PROPERTIES OF STRAIGHT-CHAIN ALKANES

Name	# of Carbons	Boiling Point (°C)	Melting Point (°C)	Density
methane	1	-162	-183	0.47
ethane	2	-89	-183	0.57
propane	3	-42	-188	0.50
butane	4	0	-138	0.58
pentane	5	36	-130	0.56
hexane	6	69	-95	0.66
heptane	7	98	-91	0.68
octane	8	126	-57	0.70
nonane	9	151	-54	0.72
decane	10	174	-30	0.74

1. The general trends shown in the chart are:

   A. as the number of carbons increases, all properties increase in value (with occasional exceptions).
   B. as the number of carbons increases, boiling points and melting points decrease, while density increases.
   C. as the number of carbons increases, density decreases and other properties increase.
   D. as the number of carbons increases, all properties decrease.

2. The change in boiling point is greatest:

   F. from methane to ethane.
   G. from propane to butane.
   H. from butane to pentane.
   J. from nonane to decane.

3. For alkanes with more than one carbon, the change in melting point from one alkane to the next:

   A. tends to be greater from an even number of carbons to the next odd number.
   B. tends to be greater from an odd number of carbons to the next even number.
   C. is similar, whether from an even number of carbons to the next odd number, or from an odd number of carbons to the next even number.
   D. Cannot be determined from the given information.

4. Considering the alkane properties listed, if alkane X has a higher boiling point than alkane Y, then without exception, it must also have a:

   F. higher melting point.
   G. higher density.
   H. higher number of carbons.
   J. longer name.

5. The greatest percentage increase in density occurs from:

   A. ethane to propane.
   B. propane to butane.
   C. pentane to hexane.
   D. hexane to heptane.

GO ON TO THE NEXT PAGE

Passage II

A student performs a set of physics laboratory experiments, in which objects of different masses glide "frictionlessly" along a smooth surface, collide, and then continue to glide. The momentum of each object is defined as its "mass • velocity." The momentum of a system of objects is the sum of the individual momentums.

Experiment 1: The light mass moves toward the stationary, heavy mass, and both stick together and continue to move. Table 1 shows the relevant information.

Table 1

	Object 1	Object 2
Mass	2 kg	5 kg
Initial velocity	4 m/sec	0 m/sec
Final velocity	1.14 m/sec	1.14 m/sec

Experiment 2: The student performs a similar experiment in which the objects do not stick together, but collide "elastically"—that is, rebound from each other with no loss in energy. Table 2 shows the results.

Table 2

	Object 1	Object 2
Mass	2 kg	5 kg
Initial velocity	4 m/sec	0 m/sec
Final velocity	-1.71 m/sec	2.29 m/sec

(Note that positive velocities indicate motion to the right, negative velocities indicate motion to the left.)

6. In Experiment 1, the momentum of Object 1 before the collision is:

   F. 0 kg • m/sec.
   G. 2 kg • m/sec.
   H. 4 kg • m/sec.
   J. 8 kg • m/sec.

7. After the collision in Experiment 1, the momentum of the combined masses is:

   A. much less than the initial total momentum of the two masses.
   B. about equal to the initial total momentum of the two masses.
   C. much greater than the initial total momentum of the two masses.
   D. Cannot be determined from the given information

8. After the collision in Experiment 2:

   F. both objects are moving to the right.
   G. both objects are moving to the left.
   H. Object 1 is moving to the left and Object 2 to the right.
   J. Object 1 is moving to the right and Object 2 to the left.

9. In Experiment 2, if Object 2 were replaced by another object that was far more massive than Object 1, its final velocity would be closest to:

   A. 4.0 m/sec.
   B. 2.3 m/sec.
   C. -1.7 m/sec.
   D. 0 m/sec.

10. Under the conditions described in the previous question, the final velocity of Object 1 would be closest to:

    F. –2 m/sec.
    G. -1.7 m/sec.
    H. 0 m/sec.
    J. 2 m/sec.

11. Kinetic energy is defined as $\frac{1}{2}(mv^2)$. During the collision described in Experiment 1, the kinetic energy of Object 1:

    A. increases.
    B. remains the same.
    C. decreases.
    D. Cannot be determined from the given information.

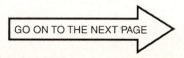

Passage III

The table below shows how an increase (+) or a decrease (-) in one or more plant hormones and environmental factors can affect various plant activities. The activities listed on the left occur when the combinations of conditions to the right exist at the same time. Hormones (H) are numbered; *e.g.*, H_1, H_2, *etc.*

Activities	H_1	H_2	H_3	H_4	H_5	Day Length	Temperature
Plant growth	+ +		+ +				
No plant growth (1)	+ +		+ +	+ +			
No plant growth (2)	+ +		+ +		+ +		
Seed germination			+ +				
Flowering			+ +		+ +	(+ + or - -)†	+ +
Flower drop-off	- -	+ +					
Fruit drop-off	- -	+ +					
Leaf drop-off	- -	+ +					- -

†Different species of plants require different combinations of light and darkness to stimulate flowering.

12. Based on the information in the table, a drop in temperature will help cause:

    F. flowering.
    G. loss of leaves, fruit, and flowers.
    H. loss of leaves only.
    J. seed germination.

13. The hormones that can inhibit (prevent) plant growth are:

    A. 1 and 3.
    B. 1, 3, and 4.
    C. 1, 3, and 5.
    D. 4 and 5.

14. Which conclusion is correct about the various factors affecting plant activities?

    F. Hormone 3 influences more plant activities than any other factor.
    G. Seed germination is influenced by the fewest factors, whereas flowering is influenced by the most.
    H. For Hormone 1 to have an effect on any plant activity, it must be changing in the opposite direction of at least one other hormone.
    J. Temperature changes can affect all plant activities.

15. Which activity would most likely be affected by changing a houseplant's growing conditions from twelve hours of light per twelve hours of darkness to constant light?

    I. Plant growth
    II. Loss of leaves
    III. Flowering

    A. I only
    B. II only
    C. III only
    D. I and III only

16. Which statement best describes the relationship between Hormone 1 and Hormone 2?

    F. Hormone 2 must change in the opposite direction of Hormone 1 for plant growth to occur.
    G. When Hormone 1 and Hormone 2 affect a plant activity together, no other factors influence that activity.
    H. As Hormone 1 increases, Hormone 2 always decreases; and as Hormone 1 decreases, Hormone 2 always increases.
    J. Hormone 2 only affects plant activities when Hormone 1 is also involved.

Passage IV

In order to examine the factors that affect the flow of substances across cell membranes, three experiments were carried out. In each experiment, semi-permeable bags (bags with small pores that allow some substances to pass through, but not others) were partially filled with a fluid, tied, and then weighed (first weighing). The bags were then submerged into a large beaker of water, and at 10-minute intervals, removed from the beaker of water and re-weighed.

Experiment 1: A bag containing a 30% red dye solution (30% red dye and 70% water) weighed 100 grams. The bag was then submerged in a beaker of pure water. After 20 minutes, the bag weighed 110 grams. The beaker water remained clear.

Experiment 2: A second bag containing 40% red dye solution (40% red dye and 60% water) weighed 100 grams before being submerged in a beaker of pure water. After only 10 minutes, the bag weighed 110 grams. The beaker water remained clear.

Experiment 3: A third bag containing only pure water and weighing 100 grams was submerged in a beaker of 50% red dye solution (50% red dye and 50% water). After 20 minutes, the bag weighed 70 grams. The bag water remained clear.

17. In Experiment 1, a gain in bag weight suggests that:

    A. material passed out from bag to beaker faster than it passed in from beaker to bag.
    B. material passed in from beaker to bag faster than it passed out from bag to beaker.
    C. material passed in and out of the bag at approximately the same rate.
    D. material did not move at all.

18. Which of the following hypotheses is supported by the results of all three experiments?

    F. Red dye can leave the bag but not enter.
    G. Red dye can enter the bag but not leave.
    H. Red dye can enter or leave the bag.
    J. Red dye cannot enter or leave the bag.

19. Which of the following represents the best approximation for the weight of the bag in Experiment 2 after 20 minutes?

    A. 90 grams
    B. 100 grams
    C. 110 grams
    D. 120 grams

20. Which of the following questions is the entire set of experiments designed to answer?

    F. How does concentration of red dye affect rate and direction of water flow?
    G. How does concentration of water affect rate and direction of red dye flow?
    H. How does rate of red dye flow affect direction of water movement?
    J. How does direction of red dye movement affect rate of water flow?

21. A control experiment was set up to confirm the investigation's conclusion. A bag containing pure water and weighing 100 grams was submerged in a beaker of pure water. What is expected to occur?

    A. The bag will slowly gain weight.
    B. The bag will slowly lose weight.
    C. The bag will remain approximately the same weight.
    D. The bag will eventually become empty, and the water level in the beaker will rise.

22. Assuming that salts cannot freely pass across a cell's membrane, what would happen to human red blood cells (approximately 1% salt and 99% water) submerged in sea water (approximately 5% salt and 95% water)?

    F. The cells would shrink due to a loss of water.
    G. The cells would shrink due to a loss of salt.
    H. The cells would swell up due to a gain of water.
    J. The cells would swell up due to a gain of salt.

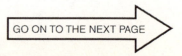

Passage V

The chart below shows various physical characteristics of different types of soil.

PHYSICAL CHARACTERISTICS OF SOIL				
Types of Soil	Diameter of Particles (μm)	Relative Ability[†] to Hold Positively Charged Minerals (Ca^{+2}, K^+, Mg^{+2})	Relative Ability[†] to Maintain Air Spaces	Relative Ability[†] to Retain Water
Clay	less than 2	1	4	1
Silt	2-20	2	3	2
Sand	20-200	3	2	3
Coarse Sand	200-2,000	4	1	4

[†]Relative abilities are rated from 1, indicating the best (most able), to 4, indicating the worst (least able).

23. The soil type that is LEAST able to hold substances such as magnesium (Mg^{+2}) is:

    A. sand.
    B. coarse sand.
    C. silt.
    D. clay.

24. Based on the information in the chart, which of the following statements best describes the relationship between a soil's particle size and its other physical characteristics?

    F. As particle size increases, the ability to hold positively charged minerals increases.
    G. As particle size decreases, the ability to retain water decreases.
    H. As particle size decreases, the ability to maintain air spaces increases.
    J. As particle size increases, the ability to retain water decreases.

25. The size of particles in the soil type that is neither best nor worst at any of the listed abilities must be:

    A. less than 20 micrometers.
    B. more than 20 micrometers.
    C. between 2 and 200 micrometers.
    D. between 2 and 2,000 micrometers.

26. Loam is a type of soil that is mostly clay, but it also contains some sand and silt particles. Which prediction is most likely to be accurate about the ability of loam to support plant growth?

    F. Plants will grow well because loam primarily has small particles that can hold minerals and retain water, yet it also has enough large particles to provide air spaces containing oxygen.
    G. Plants will grow well because loam primarily has large particles that can provide air spaces containing oxygen, yet it also has enough small particles that can hold minerals and retain water.
    H. Plants will not grow well because although loam is excellent at maintaining air spaces for oxygen, it will not hold enough minerals or water.
    J. Plants will not grow well because although loam has enough minerals and air spaces for oxygen, it cannot retain enough water.

27. Based on the information provided in the chart, which of the following conclusions about soil types is NOT correct?

    A. Soils best at retaining water are also best at holding positively charged minerals.
    B. No two soil types have the exact same combination of relative abilities.
    C. Clay and coarse sand are the soil types that are most different in every physical characteristic.
    D. At each listed ability, a different type of soil is best.

Passage VI

Theory 1: The rate of a chemical reaction is defined as the number of moles of a specified reactant consumed in one second. Reactants must collide in order for a reaction to occur, so it might seem that rates would depend upon the concentration of reactants—the more reactants that are present, the greater the likelihood of a collision. In fact, this is the case; a concrete example makes this clear. For the reaction: $2NO + O_2 \Rightarrow 2NO_2$, the rate is proportional to the amount of NO and O_2 present. This fact is expressed as the following "rate law": rate = $k[NO]^2[O_2]^1$, where k is the rate constant, and the exponents reflect the coefficients in front of the reactants in the reaction. The relationship between numbers of reactant molecules and exponents in the rate law is a general one.

Theory 2: Theory 1 is very often true, for it expresses the reasonable insight that the greater the concentration of reactants, the greater the likelihood of a reaction. It has a great shortcoming, however, in its assumption that all reactions proceed in one fell swoop rather than in several skirmishes.

For example, let letters A, B, and C stand for molecules. In the reaction $A + 2B \Rightarrow C$, Theory 1 predicts a rate law as follows: rate = $k[A][B]^2$. However, if the reaction actually proceeds in two stages, the first one would be $A + B \Rightarrow AB$ and the second one would be $AB + B \Rightarrow C$.

Thus, Theory 2 implies that one must understand the details of the reaction, including the relative speeds of the sub-reactions, in order to predict a rate law. Theory 1 is not completely wrong, just incomplete.

28. Theory 1 relates:

    F. reaction rate to the concentration of products.
    G. reaction rate to the concentration of reactants.
    H. the relative amounts of products to one other.
    J. reaction rate to the individual rates of various stages of the reaction.

29. According to a proponent of Theory 2, Theory 1:

    A. can never give a correct prediction for a rate law.
    B. will give a correct result if the reactant coefficients are all equal to 1.
    C. will give a correct result for a single-stage reaction.
    D. is in error because it claims that collisions are required for reactions to occur.

30. According to Theory 1, the rate of the reaction $3M + 2N \Rightarrow 4P$ will be given by:

    F. $k[M][N]$.
    G. $k[M]^3[N]^2$.
    H. $k[M]^3[N]^2[P]^4$.
    J. $k([M]^3 + [N]^2)$.

31. A chemist studies the rate of the reaction $2NO_2 + F_2 \Rightarrow 2NO_2F$. According to Theory 1, the rate of the reaction is proportional to:

    A. the first power of NO_2 and the first power of F_2.
    B. the second power of NO_2 and the second power of NO_2F.
    C. the second power of NO_2 and the second power of F_2.
    D. the second power of NO_2 and the first power of F_2.

32. Supporters of Theory 2 would best be able to defend their positions if:

    F. they could show that the reaction occurs in more than one stage.
    G. they slowed the reaction down by cooling the reactants.
    H. they sped the reaction up with additional heat.
    J. they eliminated all collisions.

33. According to Theory 2, if in a two-stage reaction Stage 1 is much slower than Stage 2, then the overall reaction rate will be:

    A. primarily determined by the rate of Stage 1.
    B. primarily determined by the rate of Stage 2.
    C. undeterminable unless all collisions are counted.
    D. undeterminable unless the rate law is measured experimentally.

34. When discussing the rates of reactions that have more than one stage, Theory 2 would not be necessary if:

    F. all stages went quickly.
    G. all stages had different rates.
    H. the sum of the rates of each stage always equaled the rate of the reaction as a whole.
    J. the sum of the rates of each stage was never equal to the rate of the reaction as a whole.

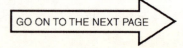

Passage VII

Closely related species of butterflies are often found living in very different environments. A pair of experiments was performed in which butterfly species previously captured in either desert areas or mountain areas were tested in laboratory incubators to determine the conditions at which they could carry out important life functions such as mating, oviposition (egg-laying), and pupation (the stage in which the stationary cocoon undergoes its final development into an adult).

Experiment 1: Under conditions of 100% relative humidity (maximum moisture content of the air), 100 desert butterflies (Species D) and 100 mountain butterflies (Species M) were tested at temperature intervals of 2° C (from 0° C to 40° C) to determine if they could mate, oviposit, and pupate. Each species achieved at least 90% success at the following ranges of temperatures:

Table 1

TEMPERATURE RANGES (° C)			
	Mating	Oviposition	Pupation
Species D	10-34	14-34	4-38
Species M	6-30	10-28	4-34

Experiment 2: The experiment was repeated at 0% relative humidity (minimum moisture content of the air). The species achieved at least 90% success at the following ranges of temperatures:

Table 2

TEMPERATURE RANGES (° C)			
	Mating	Oviposition	Pupation
Species D	10-34	14-34	4-38
Species M	6-24	10-22	4-28

35. Results of Experiments 1 and 2 indicate that the life function with the narrowest range of temperature at which both species achieve 90% success is:

   A. mating.
   B. oviposition.
   C. pupation.
   D. different in Experiment 1 than it is in Experiment 2.

36. Which condition has the most detrimental effects on Species M for mating, oviposition, and pupation?

   F. Moist air at low temperatures
   G. Moist air at high temperatures
   H. Dry air at low temperatures
   J. Dry air at high temperatures

37. A third experiment was conducted at 100% relative humidity in which the temperature range for caterpillar survival (another life function) was tested in Species D and Species M. Species D achieved 90% success at 12-36 (° C), while Species M achieved 90% success at 8-30 (° C). Which temperature range is a good prediction of survival in Species D under dry conditions?

   A. 8° C-30° C
   B. 8° C-24° C
   C. 12° C-36° C
   D. 12° C-30° C

38. If an investigator wanted to set up an experiment to determine the effects of light and dark on mating ability in Species D and Species M at 100% relative humidity, which set of conditions would provide the most complete results?

   F. Test both species at 6° C in the light and 6° C in the dark.
   G. Test both species at 20° C in the light and 20° C in the dark.
   H. Test both species at 34° C in the light and 34° C in the dark.
   J. Test both species at 34° C in the light and 30° C in the dark.

39. Which hypothesis is NOT supported by the results of Experiment 1 and Experiment 2?

   A. For all tested life functions, dry conditions only affect Species M at the high end of its temperature ranges.
   B. For all tested life functions, dry conditions have no effects on the temperature ranges of the desert species.
   C. Species D does better than Species M at high temperatures in all tested life functions.
   D. Species M does better than Species D at low temperatures for pupation.

STEP FOUR

40. Which of the following statements best explains the broad range of temperatures for pupation observed in both butterfly species?

    F. Since the cocoon is stationary, it must be able to survive changing temperature conditions until the adult butterfly emerges.
    G. Deserts can get very hot and mountains can get very cold.
    H. Mountain butterflies would not survive long in the desert, and desert butterflies would not survive long in the mountains.
    J. The stationary cocoon must be able to survive under light and dark conditions until the adult butterfly emerges.

ACT • PLAN • EXPLORE
SCIENCE REASONING

ACT SCIENCE REASONING
PRACTICE TEST II

PRACTICE TEST II

SCIENCE REASONING
35 Minutes—40 Questions

DIRECTIONS: There are seven passages in this test. Each passage is followed by several questions. After reading a passage, choose the best answer to each question and fill in the corresponding oval on your answer document. You may refer to the passages as often as necessary. You are NOT permitted to use a calculator on this test. Answers are on page 211.

Passage I

The table below shows selected elements from the periodic table, together with atomic radii in angstrom units (Å) and electronegativities (second number). When two atoms form a covalent bond, the approximate bond length may be calculated by adding together the two atomic radii.

H 0.37 Å 2.20						
Li 1.35 Å 0.98	Be 0.90 Å 1.57	B 0.80 Å 2.04	C 0.77 Å 2.55	N 0.70 Å 3.04	O 0.66 Å 3.44	F 0.64 Å 3.98
Na 1.54 Å 0.93	Mg 1.30 Å 1.31	Al 1.25 Å 1.61	Si 1.17 Å 1.90	P 1.10 Å 2.19	S 1.04 Å 2.58	Cl 0.99 Å 3.16
K 1.96 Å 0.82						Br 1.14 Å 2.96
Rb 2.11 Å 0.82						I 1.33 Å 2.66

The electronegativity has important chemical significance. If two atoms form a bond, the difference in the two electronegativities indicates the degree to which the bond is covalent (indicated by a small difference) or ionic (indicated by a large difference).

1. What occurs when moving down the table's columns?

   A. Radii decrease; electronegativities decrease.
   B. Radii increase; electronegativities increase.
   C. Radii decrease; electronegativities increase.
   D. Radii increase; electronegativities decrease.

2. The greatest electronegativity in the table is:

   F. fluorine (F).
   G. chlorine (Cl).
   H. rubidium (Rb).
   J. hydrogen (H).

3. The bond length in the P-Cl bond is:

   A. 0.11 angstroms.
   B. 0.97 angstroms.
   C. 2.09 angstroms.
   D. 5.35 angstroms.

4. The bond between which of the following is likely to have the most covalent character?

   F. Sodium (Na) and iodine (I)
   G. Magnesium (Mg) and oxygen (O)
   H. Sulfur (S) and oxygen (O)
   J. Carbon (C) and nitrogen (N)

5. The table indicates that bonds of greatest ionic character generally occur:

   A. between elements by each other in a row.
   B. between elements that are near each other in a column but far apart along a row.
   C. between elements that are far apart along a column but close in a row.
   D. between elements far apart along a column and far apart in a row.

6. The element cesium (Cs) lies directly below rubidium (Rb) in the Periodic Table. The electronegativity difference in CsF is likely to be:

   F. less than 3.16.
   G. equal to 3.16.
   H. greater than 3.16.
   J. Cannot be determined from the given information

GO ON TO THE NEXT PAGE

STEP FOUR

Passage II

A set of experiments was carried out to investigate the relative sizes of the planets of our solar system and the relative distances from the Sun. Table 1 was given to all students performing the experiments.

Experiment 1: Using a compass, ruler, and paper (11 in. × 14 in.), students were asked to compare the sizes of the planets. Calling the size of Earth 1.00 (Earth diameter = 5 in.), a circle was made by inserting the point of the compass in the center of the paper. The circle had a radius of 2.5 in. to produce a circle with a diameter of 5 in. representing the Earth. All other planets were drawn to scale based on the size of their diameters relative to one Earth diameter (Table 1).

Table 1

Planet	Approximate Diameter (in Earth diameters)	Approximate Distance from the Sun (A.U.)
Mercury	0.38	0.40
Venus	0.95	0.70
Earth	1.00	1.00
Mars	0.54	1.50
Jupiter	11.20	5.20
Saturn	9.50	9.50
Uranus	3.70	19.20
Neptune	3.50	30.00
Pluto	0.47	40.00

Experiment 2: Using the equipment from Experiment 1, students were also asked to compare planetary distances from the Sun. The Earth is 93 million miles from the Sun. This distance is called 1.00 Astronomical Unit (1 A.U. = 0.5 inches), and it was used as a reference distance when the other planets were drawn at their proper distances (Table 1) from the Sun (a planet twice as far as the Earth is from the Sun would be drawn 2 A.U., or 1.0 inches, from the Sun).

7. In Experiment 1, the two planets represented by circles most similar in size on the paper are:

    A. Earth and Venus.
    B. Mars and Pluto.
    C. Uranus and Neptune.
    D. Mercury and Pluto.

8. In Experiment 2, if the paper were held the "long way" and the left-hand paper edge represented the Sun, which planet(s) would not fit on the paper?

    F. Uranus, Neptune, and Pluto
    G. Neptune and Pluto
    H. Pluto only
    J. All planets would fit on the paper.

9. Which of the following statements is supported by the data in Table 1?

    A. The larger the planet, the greater is its distance from the Sun.
    B. The smaller the planet, the greater is its distance from the Sun.
    C. Only planets larger than the Earth are farther away from the Sun.
    D. There is no consistent pattern between a planet's size and its distance from the Sun.

10. A planet's "year" is how long it takes to orbit the Sun and it is related to the distance of that planet from the Sun. If asteroids are found 2.8 A.U. from the Sun, an "asteroid year" should be:

    F. longer than a "Mars year" but shorter than a "Jupiter year."
    G. longer than an "Earth year" but shorter than a "Mars year."
    H. longer than an "Earth year" but shorter than a "Neptune year."
    J. longer than a "Neptune year" but shorter than a "Uranus year."

11. In Experiment 1, how large would a circle representing the Sun be if its diameter is approximately 110 times greater than that of the Earth?

    A. It would have a radius of approximately 550 inches.
    B. It would have a diameter of approximately 550 inches.
    C. It would have a radius of approximately 55 inches.
    D. It would have a diameter of approximately 55 inches.

12. A third experiment was conducted in which the mass of each planet was described relative to the mass of the Earth (Jupiter had the greatest mass, Saturn had the next largest mass, Mercury and Pluto had the smallest masses). If the planets were placed in an order based on how they compared to Earth for the variables measured in all three experiments, which two orders would be expected to be most similar?

    F. Diameter and distance from the Sun
    G. Mass and distance from the Sun
    H. Diameter and mass
    J. All three orders would be similar.

Passage III

It is known that during photosynthesis, leaf pigments absorb light energy that eventually results in the production of glucose and other carbohydrates to be used by the green plant. Oxygen gas (O_2) is also produced during the process. Various factors affecting the rate of photosynthesis were investigated by counting the number of oxygen bubbles produced under the conditions described in the following three experiments.

Experiment 1: A sample of leaf extract (a mixture of pigments previously separated from other leaf components) from the pond plant *Elodea* was placed in a beaker containing water and a standard concentration of carbon dioxide (CO_2) (both are necessary ingredients for photosynthesis). Light of varying intensity was used to illuminate the beaker, and the number of oxygen bubbles emitted by the plant each minute was recorded. The results are illustrated in Figure 1.

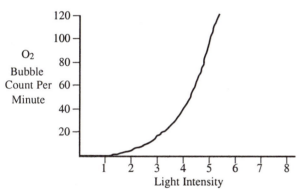

Figure 1

Experiment 2: An identical experiment was conducted in which the concentration of leaf extract was reduced four-fold (the mixture was one-fourth as concentrated as in Experiment 1). The results are shown in Figure 2.

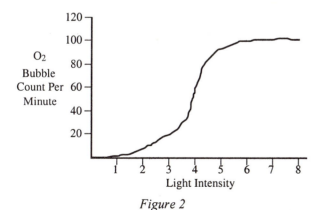

Figure 2

Experiment 3: Visible light consists of many different colors, or light wavelengths. Only those wavelengths that are absorbed by leaf pigments can provide the energy to maintain photosynthesis in the leaf. Different light wavelengths were used separately to illuminate two samples of leaf extract, each containing a different *Elodea* leaf pigment. Oxygen (O_2) bubbles were counted again as a measure of the rate of photosynthesis. Figure 3 summarizes the results.

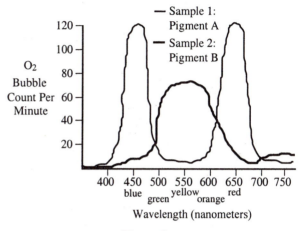

Figure 3

13. When running Experiment 1, which of the following changes in CO_2 should be made in order to determine its effect on the rate of photosynthesis?

    A. Repeat the experiment using the same concentration of CO_2 in the beaker of water, but with different species of green plants.
    B. Repeat the experiment using first no CO_2 and then varying concentrations of carbon dioxide in the beaker of water.
    C. Repeat the experiment using different levels of water in the beaker containing a standard concentration of CO_2.
    D. Repeat the experiment using additional light intensities.

14. The results in Experiments 1 and 2 demonstrate that in order to maintain a continued increase in the photosynthesis rate:

    F. adequate amounts of light are needed.
    G. adequate amounts of carbon dioxide are needed.
    H. adequate amounts of oxygen are needed.
    J. adequate amounts of leaf pigments are needed.

15. Based on the information in Figure 3, which of the following statements is correct?

    A. Pigment A primarily absorbs light at 450 and 650 nanometers, while Pigment B absorbs light at 500-575 nanometers.
    B. Pigment B primarily absorbs light at 450 and 650 nanometers, while Pigment A primarily absorbs light at 500-575 nanometers.
    C. Pigment A can influence the rate of photosynthesis, while Pigment B cannot.
    D. Pigment B can influence the rate of photosynthesis, while Pigment A cannot.

16. If the concentration of *Elodea* leaf extract was increased in Experiment 2, which of the following results could be expected?

    F. A decrease in the number of oxygen bubbles
    G. An increase in the number of oxygen bubbles
    H. No change in the number of oxygen bubbles
    J. A gradual dimming of light intensity

17. In Experiments 1 and 2, approximately how many oxygen bubbles/minute were produced at a light intensity level of 4?

    A. 20-30
    B. 30-40
    C. 40-50
    D. Between 0 and 10

18. According to the information in Figure 3, if an additional experiment were conducted, which condition would be LEAST effective in maintaining photosynthetic rate in *Elodea*?

    F. Using blue light only
    G. Using red light only
    H. Using yellow light only
    J. Using orange light only

Passage IV

The accompanying figure shows how the world records for various footraces have improved during a portion of this century. Speeds are given in both meters/minute and minutes/mile.

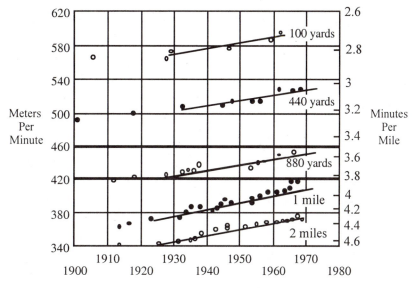

Modified from H.W. Ryder, H.J. Carr, and P. Herget, "Future performance in footracing," *Sci. Amer.* 234 (6): 109-114, 1976.

19. In what race and in what year was the greatest speed in meters/minute achieved?

    A. The 440-yard dash in 1900
    B. The 100-yard dash in 1930
    C. The 100-yard dash in 1962
    D. The 1-mile run in 1947

20. The trend in the graphs of meters/minute for the various distances shows:

    F. roughly a linear increase.
    G. roughly a linear decrease.
    H. a linear increase for short distances and a linear decrease for long distances.
    J. no systematic pattern.

21. For 1960, the ratio of minutes/mile values for the 1-mile run to that for the 440-yard dash is roughly:

    A. 3/4.
    B. 4/5.
    C. 5/4.
    D. 4/3.

22. The increase in speed, in meters/minute, for the 2-mile run from 1925 to 1967 is roughly:

    F. 0.3.
    G. 10.
    H. 30.
    J. 100.

23. If the trends shown can be expected to hold for later years, then the value of minutes per mile for the 880-yard run in 1980 is expected to be:

    A. 3.5.
    B. 3.8.
    C. 420.
    D. 460.

Passage V

Two experiments were performed in which constant amounts of heat were added continuously to samples over a defined period of time. The temperatures of the samples were monitored while the heat was added. The results from the two experiments are shown below.

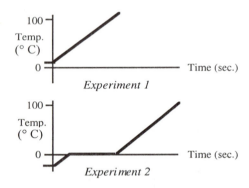

24. The results of Experiment 1 may be interpreted to show that:

    F. it takes longer to heat a hot sample than a cold one.
    G. the temperature of the sample rises proportionately with time as heat is applied.
    H. temperature is not related to heat.
    J. temperature and time measure the same thing.

25. Experiment 2 differs from Experiment 1 in that:

    A. only the starting temperature is different in the two experiments.
    B. the graph in Experiment 2 is not a straight line; there must have been experimental error.
    C. Experiment 2 has a lower starting temperature and a time period when the temperature does not rise.
    D. in Experiment 2, the heat went off for a while in the middle of the experiment.

26. The experimenter wants to explain the flat part of the graph from Experiment 2. It could represent:

    F. a period when the clock was turned off.
    G. a period when the heat was turned off.
    H. a period when heat was added but some process that did not occur in the first experiment (such as absorption of heat), caused the temperature to remain constant.
    J. a period when less heat was added.

27. The "phase" of the sample changes (an example of a phase change is the melting of a solid, or the boiling of a liquid) in conjunction with the flat part of the graph in Experiment 2. From the temperature data given, the phase change might be:

    A. the boiling of water.
    B. the melting of ice.
    C. the melting of iron.
    D. the boiling of iron.

28. The results of these experiments demonstrate that:

    F. heat and temperature are basically the same.
    G. heat and temperature are not the same.
    H. a pause in heating can lead to a pause in temperature change.
    J. constant heating leads to constant change.

29. If the experimenter extends Experiment 2 to higher temperatures, using water as a sample, which graph best illustrates the expected results?

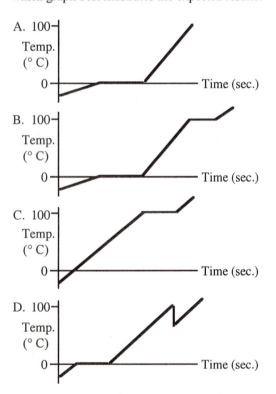

Passage VI

The following chart shows the generalized sequence of early developmental stages (terms in boxes) observed in most vertebrates.

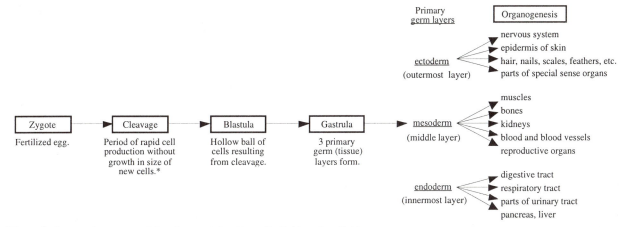

*New cells form as the zygote and its subsequent daughter cells divide and re-divide.

30. According to the chart, the stage of development when the three primary tissue layers form is:

F. cleavage.
G. blastula.
H. gastrula.
J. organogenesis.

31. Differentiation refers to a period of cell maturation during which time cells become specialized in structure and function. At which stage of development would most differentiation be expected to occur?

A. Cleavage
B. Blastula
C. Gastrula
D. Organogenesis

32. Based on the information in the diagram, which conclusion is NOT correct?

F. Vertebrates develop three primary germ layers.
G. Most bones develop from the innermost primary germ layer.
H. Diverse structures such as scales, feathers, and hair always develop from the same primary germ layer.
J. Before an organism can form different primary tissue layers, it must go through a stage in which it is in the form of a hollow ball of cells.

33. If a species of monkey were found to have extraordinary vision due to special receptor cells that were highly sensitive to different colors of light, from which primary germ layer(s) would you predict such cells to develop?

A. Endoderm
B. Mesoderm
C. Ectoderm
D. A combination of endoderm and mesoderm

34. On the basis of the information provided, the stage of development that probably has the smallest cells is:

F. zygote.
G. cleavage.
H. gastrula.
J. adult.

Passage VII

The following are two theories regarding the proportions of chemicals that will react to form products.

Theory 1: Although a chemical reaction is more than simple mixing, the two are similar in that any amounts of reactants may be brought together to form chemical products that contain the same elements as the reactants. For example, in the reaction "hydrogen + oxygen $\Rightarrow$ water" we may use 1 mole of hydrogen and 1 mole of oxygen, or 2 to 1, or 1 to 2, *etc*. The reaction will adjust to the proportions given.

Theory 2: Only certain proportions of reactants will combine chemically. For example, when hydrogen and oxygen are reacted, the amounts that will combine will be *exactly* 2 grams of hydrogen for every 32 grams of oxygen. We can show, using molecular weights, that these weights of reactants (which correspond to 2 moles of hydrogen and 1 mole of oxygen), imply the following reaction:

$$2H_2 + O_2 \Rightarrow 2H_2O$$

From this statement about the proportions of hydrogens and oxygens that react with each other, we can conclude that two hydrogen molecules must react with a single oxygen molecule to form two molecules of water.

35. Theory 1 does NOT predict which of the following?

    A. 2 moles of zinc may react completely with 2 moles of sulfur.
    B. 2 moles of zinc may react completely with 3 moles of sulfur.
    C. 7 moles of zinc may react completely with 4 moles of sulfur.
    D. If 3 moles of zinc were mixed with 4 moles of sulfur, 1 mole of sulfur would be left unreacted.

36. According to Theory 1, how many moles of water would be produced by the reaction of 2 moles of hydrogen and 1 mole of oxygen?

    F. 1
    G. 2
    H. 4
    J. Cannot be determined from the given information

37. An experimenter finds that when 170 grams of $AgNO_3$ is reacted with 58.5 grams of NaCl to form products, none of the original reactants remain in appreciable amounts. When the original amount of $AgNO_3$ is increased to 175 grams, then all of the NaCl is used up, but 5 grams of $AgNO_3$ remains. This result is:

    A. consistent with Theory 1.
    B. consistent with Theory 2.
    C. consistent with both Theory 1 and Theory 2.
    D. not consistent with either theory.

38. According to Theory 2, how might the remaining 5 grams of $AgNO_3$ be used up?

    F. Add more of the reactant NaCl.
    G. Remove some of the reactant NaCl.
    H. Add even more of the reactant $AgNO_3$.
    J. There is no mechanism for using the 5 grams of $AgNO_3$.

39. An experimenter wishes to determine which theory better fits her data for an experiment in which iron (Fe) is chemically combined with oxygen (O). She finds that 2 moles of Fe will react completely with 2 moles of O; she also finds that 2 moles of Fe will react completely with 3 moles of O. At this point she is confident that Theory 1, which is in opposition to the idea of "definite proportions," is correct. What further experiment might she do to test the success of Theory 1 over Theory 2?

    A. Add 1 mole of Fe to 1 mole of O.
    B. Add 2 moles of Fe to 4 moles of O.
    C. Add 3 moles of Fe to 4.5 moles of O.
    D. Add 4 moles of Fe to 4 moles of O.

40. According to Theory 1, the product of the reaction of hydrogen and oxygen:

    F. is H_2O.
    G. could be anything.
    H. must contain hydrogen and oxygen, but lacks a specific formula.
    J. has a definite proportion of hydrogen to oxygen.

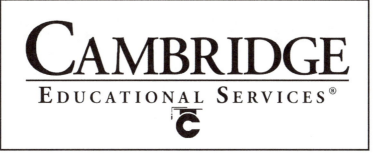

ACT • PLAN • EXPLORE SCIENCE REASONING

ACT SCIENCE REASONING PRACTICE TEST III

SCIENCE REASONING
35 Minutes—40 Questions

DIRECTIONS: There are seven passages in this test. Each passage is followed by several questions. After reading a passage, choose the best answer to each question and fill in the corresponding oval on your answer document. You may refer to the passages as often as necessary. You are NOT permitted to use a calculator on this test. Answers are on page 214.

Passage I

Before making their historic first powered flight, the Wright Brothers made extensive lift tests in 1901 using a glider. Their data differed from that obtained twelve years earlier by the German, Otto Lilienthal.

Results of both tests (Wright: thin line; Lilienthal: thick line) are shown below. "Lift" is the force that pulls the wing away from the Earth, in a direction perpendicular to the flight path, and the "angle of incidence" is the angle that the flight path makes with the horizon.

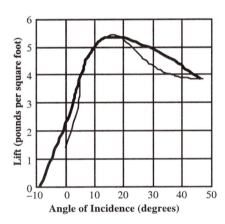

Modified from Culick, F.E.C, "The Wright 'Flyer' was the outcome of an intensive program of research." *Sci. Amer. 241* (1): 86-100, 1979.

1. The two curves differ chiefly in that:

   A. the Wright's data were more accurate.
   B. lift was generally greater in the Wright's experiments.
   C. lift was generally greater in Lilienthal's experiments.
   D. the peak value for lift was greater in Lilienthal's experiments.

2. In the Wright's experiments, the greatest lift occurred at an angle of incidence of about:

   F. 5.5 degrees.
   G. 0 degrees.
   H. 16 degrees.
   J. 46 degrees.

3. At an angle of incidence of 50 degrees, by how much would you expect the two experiments to show a difference in lift?

   A. 0-1 pounds/sq. ft.
   B. 1-2 pounds/sq. ft.
   C. 2-3 pounds/sq. ft.
   D. 3-4 pounds/sq. ft.

4. The two sets of experiments differed most in lift at which of the following angles?

   F. 10 degrees
   G. 15 degrees
   H. 30 degrees
   J. 40 degrees

5. The widest range of angles, in degrees, over which the Lilienthal values for lift continuously exceeded the Wright's values was:

   A. 10.
   B. 19.
   C. 25.
   D. 43.

GO ON TO THE NEXT PAGE

Passage II

Two experiments were performed to determine the effects of temperature on the rate of cellular respiration* in germinating peas.

*Summary Equation: $C_6H_{12}O_6 + 6O_2 \Rightarrow 6CO_2 + 6H_2O$
(glucose) (oxygen) (carbon dioxide) (water)

Experiment 1: A simple respirometer was used, primarily consisting of a large test tube partially filled with germinating peas. The peas were covered with a layer of cotton and a small amount of potassium hydroxide (KOH), a substance that can absorb and remove carbon dioxide from the tube. The remainder of the tube, with its starting volume of air sealed inside (200 ml.), was closed to the outside with a rubber stopper. Attached was a meter designed to detect and measure any changes in gas volume in the tube during the experiment. The experiment was conducted at room temperature (22° C), and the respirator was monitored for 15 minutes. At the end of 15 minutes, the volume of gas inside the tube had *decreased* to 120 ml.

Experiment 2: An identical experiment was conducted at 30° C. At this temperature, the volume of gas inside the tube after 15 minutes had decreased from 200 ml (starting volume) to 60 ml.

6. Separate control experiments were performed alongside Experiments 1 and 2. The control contained plastic beads (the same size as peas) instead of germinating peas. All other conditions were identical. Any decrease in gas volume inside the control tube would suggest that:

F. plastic beads utilize oxygen at approximately the same rate as germinating peas.
G. plastic beads produce carbon dioxide at about the same rate as germinating peas.
H. plastic beads carry out all aspects of cellular respiration at approximately the same rate as germinating peas.
J. factors having nothing to do with cellular respiration must be responsible.

7. In both experiments, the decrease in volume in the tube was mainly due to a change in the volume of what specific gas?

A. Oxygen
B. Carbon dioxide
C. Potassium hydroxide
D. All of the above

8. If potassium hydroxide (KOH) were not included in the tubes, what would happen to the volume of gas during each experiment?

F. Final volumes would be higher than starting volumes.
G. Final volumes would decrease faster than what was observed in Experiments 1 and 2.
H. Final volumes would approximately be the same as starting volumes.
J. Results would not be different from what was observed in Experiments 1 and 2.

9. Experiment 2 showed a greater decrease in gas volume in the tube because:

A. at higher temperatures, peas use oxygen slower.
B. at higher temperatures, peas produce carbon dioxide faster.
C. at higher temperatures, peas use oxygen faster.
D. at lower temperatures, peas use oxygen slower than they produce carbon dioxide.

10. An additional set of experiments with germinating peas is conducted in the dark at 22° C and 30° C. All other conditions are identical to those in Experiments 1 and 2. After 15 minutes, if the final gas volume inside the tube at 22° C is 120 ml, and the final gas volume inside the tube at 30° C is 60 ml, which hypothesis best explains the results?

F. Darkness affects cellular respiration in germinating peas the same way that a rise in temperature affects cellular respiration in germinating peas.
G. Light/dark conditions have little or no effect on cellular respiration in germinating peas.
H. Cellular respiration in germinating peas occurs faster in the light than in the dark.
J. Cellular respiration in germinating peas occurs faster in the dark than in the light.

11. The summary equation in the passage shows that during cellular respiration, germinating peas must consume glucose. In Experiments 1 and 2, glucose molecules:

A. were in the peas.
B. were not available.
C. were consumed at equal rates.
D. were available but not consumed at all.

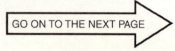

Passage III

Two different views of the Earth's past are presented below.

Scientist 1: The history of our planet has been marked by sudden spectacular events that have no counterpart in the natural processes observed today (Catastrophism). Today's valleys formed during periods of downward slippage by fragments of the Earth's crust. Mountains rose due to gigantic upheavals of land during the Earth's beginnings. The three major types of rock formed when one worldwide ocean precipitated out great masses of different materials during three sudden and separate events. Substances such as granite were precipitated first (today's igneous rocks), while materials in the flat upper layers precipitated last (today's sedimentary rocks). This was followed by the disappearance of much of this great ocean's water (perhaps by evaporation during years of intensive heat). Distinct assemblages of animal and plant fossils, found in successive rock layers of a region, can be explained by local catastrophic events, such as massive fires or floods. Old forms were wiped out, and eventually new forms replaced them as foreign species immigrated from other geographic areas.

Scientist 2: Processes now in operation are adequate to account for changes in the Earth's past (Principle of Uniform Change). Although today's processes seem to have negligible effects on the landscape, great changes can result from ongoing processes, if given long enough periods of time. Valleys form as flowing water cuts through the sides and bottom of the land and rock they pass across. Rocks and mountains can be formed, destroyed and reformed by processes still going on today such as volcanic activity, heat and pressure under the Earth's surfaces, erosion, weathering, and even shifts and movements that can lift massive areas below the land and ocean surfaces to high elevations. Different fossil types in successive layers of rocks represent the changes in form that can take place among related organisms as a result of evolutionary processes over vast periods of time.

12. One major difference between the views of Scientist 1 and Scientist 2 relates to:

    F. where fossils are found.
    G. when the processes that shape the Earth take place.
    H. the size of mountain ranges.
    J. whether water played a role in forming any of the Earth's characteristics.

13. Which of the following provides the strongest evidence against Scientist 1's point about mountain formation?

    A. The beginnings of the Earth are not well documented.
    B. Floods and fires have never been massive enough to eliminate fossils from all mountain areas.
    C. Volcanic activity, weathering, and erosion are believed to be less common today than in years past.
    D. Fossils of recent sea creatures can be found in rocks on mountain peaks.

14. Based on the differences between Scientist 1 and Scientist 2 stated above, which description is most accurate concerning their views about the time span needed for the Earth's geologic characteristics to form?

    F. Scientist 1 makes references to time span and suggests a longer Earth history than Scientist 2.
    G. Scientist 2 makes no references to time span, but implies a shorter Earth history than Scientist 1.
    H. Scientist 2 makes references to time span and suggests a longer Earth history than does Scientist 1.
    J. Neither scientist refers to time span or implies any difference in length of Earth history.

15. According to Scientist 1, which of the major types of rocks should be found at the lowest levels?

    A. Igneous (granite)
    B. Metamorphic (marble)
    C. Sedimentary (limestone)
    D. Cannot be determined from the given information

16. According to the views of Scientist 1, the number of major rock types will most likely:

    F. remain unchanged.
    G. decrease.
    H. increase.
    J. Cannot be determined from the given information

17. To refute Scientist 2's point of view about strictly uniform processes of change, Scientist 1 could argue that:

    A. the streams of today are not measurably effective in cutting through the sides and bottoms of rock they pass across.
    B. fossils are not found everywhere today.
    C. at some early point in time, the actual formation of the Earth had to involve very different processes from those now in evidence.
    D. no mountain ranges have formed in our lifetime.

18. Which argument does NOT support the views of Scientist 2?

    F. There are many regions of lava where no volcanoes are present today.
    G. There are three major types of rock that exist today.
    H. Many rivers today are flowing far below their former channels.
    J. Distinctive fossils in upper layers of rock show similarities to those in lower layers, yet they are never found in any other geographic areas.

Passage IV

Cold-blooded animals (poikilotherms) cannot regulate their body temperatures internally. Their body temperature varies as the environmental temperature varies. Consequently, the rates of many bodily processes also vary as outside temperatures change (as environmental temperatures increase, body temperature as well as the rates of bodily processes also may increase). Warm-blooded animals (homeotherms), on the other hand, can maintain their body temperatures internally. Therefore, the rates of their bodily processes can remain relatively stable when environmental temperatures change.

Experiments were set up to determine how the bodily process heart rate may be affected by different temperatures in two species of live laboratory animals.

Experiment 1: Ten individuals from Species A and ten individuals from Species B were kept in 20 separate containers at room temperature (22° C) for 30 minutes. Their heart rates (heart beats/minute) were recorded every 10 minutes. Average heart rates for the entire experiment were then calculated for each species. Results were as follows: Species A had an average heart rate of 150 beats/minute, while Species B averaged 100 beats/minute.

Experiment 2: Identical procedures were used to repeat the original experiment except that the containers holding the individuals of each species were placed in an incubator set at 35° C. At the end of 30 minutes, the average heart rate for both species was 148 beats/minute.

19. How many values were used to calculate the average heart beats for each species in each of these experiments?

    A. 1
    B. 10
    C. 20
    D. 30

20. Which of the following hypotheses is supported by the results of both experiments?

    F. Species A is most likely poikilothermic.
    G. Species B is most likely poikilothermic.
    H. Both species are most likely poikilothermic.
    J. Neither species is poikilothermic.

21. Which of the following statements best explains why ten individuals of each species were used in the experiments?

    A. In case a few died, there would still be others available for testing.
    B. If only one individual was used, it would be lonely.
    C. An average value for ten individuals reduces the chance of getting an extreme value for any one individual.
    D. If only one individual was chosen from each species, it would be difficult to show differences.

22. If a third experiment were conducted at 6° C, which set of results for average heart rates (in beats/minute) is closest to what might be expected?

    F. Species A = 146; Species B = 146
    G. Species A = 50; Species B = 146
    H. Species A = 50; Species B = 50
    J. Species A = 146; Species B = 50

23. Which statement is accurate concerning Species A and Species B?

    A. At 22° C, Species A has a higher average heart rate than Species B.
    B. Species A has a larger average size than Species B.
    C. As environmental temperature increases, average heart rate increases more for Species A than Species B.
    D. As environmental temperature decreases, average heart rate increases more for Species A than Species B.

24. If the average body temperature for ten individuals of each species were recorded during Experiments 1 and 2, which results would be expected?

    F. Species A: Temperature stays the same in both experiments. Species B: Temperature increases in Experiment 2.
    G. Species A: Temperature increases in Experiment 2. Species B: Temperature stays the same in both experiments.
    H. Both Species: Temperature increases in Experiment 2.
    J. Both Species: Temperature stays the same in both experiments.

Passage V

The chart below shows a set of "energy levels" that an electron in molecule X can occupy. The value of the energy in each level is shown to the right.

Energy Levels
E_5---------2.07
E_4---------1.75
E_3---------1.52
E_2---------1.20
E_1---------0.60

An electron can move from one level to the next (transition) in two ways:

(a) the molecule can absorb a particle of light, called a "photon," of just the right energy to lift the electron to a higher level. For example, an electron in level 4 can be raised to level 5 if the molecule absorbs a photon whose energy is 0.32.

(b) the molecule can emit, or give off, a photon of just the right energy necessary to lower an electron to another level. For example, an electron in level 4 can move to level 3 if the molecule emits a photon whose energy is 0.23.

25. A sample containing many X molecules absorbs light, each photon of which carries 0.60 units of energy. As the light is absorbed:

   A. an electron moves from level 1 to level 2.
   B. an electron moves from level 2 to level 4.
   C. an electron moves from level 2 to level 1.
   D. an electron moves from level 4 to level 2.

26. A sample of molecule X emits light, each photon of which carries 0.32 units of energy. Which of the following statements best explains this observation?

   F. An electron moved from level 3 to level 2.
   G. An electron moved from level 2 to level 3.
   H. An electron moved from level 5 to level 4.
   J. An electron moved from level 3 to level 2 or from level 5 to level 4.

27. A sample of molecule X emits light whose photons each carry 0.92 units of energy. As the light is emitted:

   A. an electron moves from level 5 to level 2.
   B. an electron moves from level 1 to level 5.
   C. an electron moves from level 1 to level 3.
   D. an electron moves from level 3 to level 1.

28. Suppose that in a sample of molecule X, all of the electrons are in level 1. Based on the information in the chart, photons of how many different energies could be absorbed by the sample?

   F. 1
   G. 2
   H. 3
   J. 4

29. Assume that each of the molecules in a sample of molecule X has only 1 electron, whose level is not known. Light is passed through the sample, and photons, each of energy 0.23, are absorbed. A very short time later, photons of the same energy are emitted. It is likely that:

   A. electrons are being promoted from level 1 to level 2.
   B. electrons are moving from level 4 to level 3, and then back again to level 4.
   C. electrons are moving from level 3 to level 4, then back again to level 3.
   D. electrons are moving from level 5 to level 4.

30. If photons whose individual energies are each 2.07 encounter a sample of molecule X, then:

   F. electrons will be promoted from level 1 to level 5.
   G. electrons will be promoted from all levels to level 5.
   H. electrons will drop from level 5 to level 1.
   J. no electron transitions will occur.

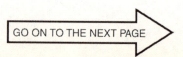

Passage VI

A student performs a set of three experiments in which a light beam passes through water and air. The "refraction angles" are the angles that the light beam makes with a vertical line. In the water, this angle is called θ_1. When the beam leaves the water and passes into air, a second angle, θ_2, can be measured. Figure 1 illustrates θ_1 and θ_2.

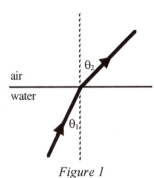

Figure 1

Experiment 1: The entry angle, θ_1, and the exit angle, θ_2, are both equal to zero.

Experiment 2: The angles observed are shown in Figure 2.

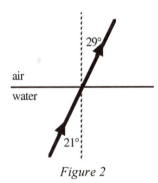

Figure 2

Experiment 3: The angles observed are shown in Figure 3.

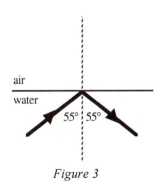

Figure 3

31. Which of the following diagrams could represent the observations of Experiment 1?

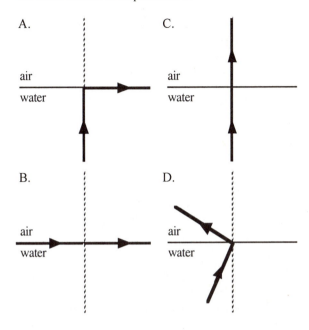

32. The student attempts to draw a conclusion from Experiments 1 and 2 that may apply to all other measurements as well. Which of the following is justified by the data?

F. Refraction angles in water are greater than those in air.
G. Refraction angles in water are less than those in air.
H. Refraction angles are equal in air and in water.
J. Refraction angles in water are equal to or less than those in air.

33. In Experiment 3, the beam travels through the water and:

A. is reflected back down from the surface of the water.
B. enters the air.
C. is absorbed completely.
D. is reflected back on itself.

34. An observer in the air attempts to see the beam of light in Experiments 2 and 3. She will:

   F. be able to observe the light in each experiment, provided she is in the right place.
   G. be unable to observe the light in either experiment, regardless of position.
   H. be able to observe the light in Experiment 2 but not Experiment 3.
   J. be able to observe the light in Experiment 3 but not Experiment 2.

35. A student attempts to summarize the results of all three experiments. Which of the following is most consistent with the observations?

   A. The angle of refraction in water is less than that in air.
   B. The angle of refraction in air is less than that in water.
   C. The angle of refraction in water is less than or equal to that in air, but at high angles in the water, the light is reflected back into the water.
   D. The angle of refraction in water is less than or equal to that in air.

Passage VII

The table below presents the results of a study in which butterflies of different size and color were captured in flight for marking with a chemical, and then recaptured in flight a few weeks later.

SIZE	WHITE		TAN		DARK BROWN	
	# marked	Recaptured	# marked	Recaptured	# marked	Recaptured
Small (less than 20 mm)	35	30	40	10	20	10
Medium (20-40 mm)	30	15	40	20	20	10
Large (greater than 40 mm)	50	25	60	30	30	10

36. For all sizes of butterflies, the color that seems most difficult to capture for marking is:

   F. white.
   G. tan.
   H. dark brown.
   J. Both tan and dark brown are almost equally difficult

37. The specific type of butterfly that is easiest to recapture after being marked is:

   A. between 10-20 mm and tan.
   B. greater than 40 mm and tan.
   C. greater than 40 mm and dark brown.
   D. less than 20 mm and white.

38. Based on the information in the table, which statement best represents the relationship between a butterfly's size and its tendency to be captured for marking?

   F. The larger the butterfly, the harder it is to be captured for marking.
   G. The larger the butterfly, the easier it is to be captured for marking.
   H. Medium-sized butterflies are consistently the easiest to capture for marking.
   J. The smaller the butterfly, the easier it is to be captured for marking.

39. The chemical used to mark all the butterflies was found to be poisonous to one specific type because it was being absorbed through the wings. Based on the data in the table, which type of butterfly appears most likely to have suffered from the effects of the marking chemical?

   A. Greater than 40 mm and white
   B. Less than 20 mm and tan
   C. Greater than 40 mm and dark brown
   D. Less than 20 mm and white

40. Which conclusion is correct concerning the information in the table?

   F. For tan butterflies, the proportion of individuals that are recaptured always stays the same.
   G. For medium-sized butterflies, the proportion of individuals that are recaptured always stays the same.
   H. For small-sized butterflies, the proportion of individuals recaptured always stays the same.
   J. For all sizes of butterflies, the darker the color the easier it is to recapture an individual.

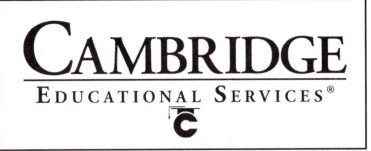

ACT • PLAN • EXPLORE
SCIENCE REASONING

ACT SCIENCE REASONING
PRACTICE TEST IV

SCIENCE REASONING
35 Minutes—40 Questions

DIRECTIONS: There are seven passages in this test. Each passage is followed by several questions. After reading a passage, choose the best answer to each question and fill in the corresponding oval on your answer document. You may refer to the passages as often as necessary. You are NOT permitted to use a calculator on this test. Answers are on page 217.

Passage I

The solubility of materials in liquids depends not only on the nature of the solute and the solvent, but also on temperature. A graph showing the solubilities of several substances in water is presented below.

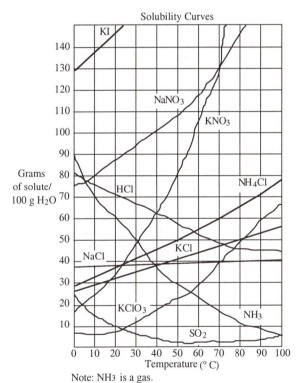

Note: NH_3 is a gas.

1. Which of the following has the most temperature sensitive solubility throughout the range shown?

   A. $NaNO_3$
   B. KNO_3
   C. $NaCl$
   D. NH_3

2. The solubility of sodium (Na) salts is:

   F. high because sodium is an alkali metal.
   G. low because sodium combines with anions to make salts.
   H. dependent on what salt it forms.
   J. always greater than 20 grams per 100 grams of water.

3. A 250 ml alcoholic solution of KNO_3 at 50° C contains how many grams KNO_3 at saturation?

   A. 80
   B. 200
   C. 30
   D. Cannot be determined from the given information

4. A solution containing equal amounts of $NaNO_3$ and KNO_3 is allowed to cool until a white powder begins to appear at the bottom of the flask. That powder is:

   F. KNO_3.
   G. $NaNO_3$.
   H. a mixture of both.
   J. Cannot be determined from the given information

5. The solubility curve of NH_3 suggests an explanation of why:

   A. divers get the bends (nitrogen bubbles in the blood) if they rise too quickly.
   B. soda goes flat.
   C. warm lemonade is sweeter than cold lemonade.
   D. hot air balloons rise.

GO ON TO THE NEXT PAGE

STEP FOUR

Passage II

Part of our understanding of the Earth comes from a consideration of its physical properties. A table of selected properties is presented below.

Property	Value
Mass	$6 \cdot 10^{24}$ kg
Diameter	$6 \cdot 10^{6}$ m
Orbital Radius	$1.5 \cdot 10^{11}$ m
Period of Revolution	365.3 days
Period of Rotation	24 hours

Below is a table comparing the other planets of the solar system to the Earth.

	Earth	Jupiter	Mars	Mercury	Neptune	Pluto	Saturn	Uranus	Venus
Diameter	1	10	0.55	0.38	4.3	?	9.4	4.1	0.98
Mass	1	320	0.10	0.58	17	?	95	14	0.83
Surface Gravity	1	2.7	0.40	0.40	1.2	?	1.2	1.1	0.90
Volume	1	1,320	0.15	0.58	42	0.729	760	50	0.90
Average Distance to Sun	1	5.3	1.5	0.40	30	40	10	19	0.70
Period of Revolution	1	12	2	0.25	165	248	30	84	0.60
Period of Rotation	1	0.40	1	60	0.50	0	0.40	0.50	240

The following are a few basic equations: (1) density = $\frac{mass}{volume}$, (2) distance = rate • time, and (3) volume of a sphere = $\frac{4}{3}\pi r^3$ where r is the radius of the sphere.

6. Based on the table above, what is the approximate ratio of the period of revolution in days to the period of rotation in days for Mercury?

   F. 240
   G. $\frac{3}{2}$
   H. $\frac{2}{3}$
   J. $\frac{1}{240}$

7. Which planet is as dense as the planet Earth?

   A. Mercury
   B. Venus
   C. Mars
   D. None

8. Which planet orbits the sun at the slowest rate?

   F. Mercury
   G. Jupiter
   H. Neptune
   J. Pluto

9. Analysis of the tables above shows that surface gravity most likely depends on:

   A. mass alone.
   B. distance and mass.
   C. density alone.
   D. density of the planet and proximity to the sun.

10. Assuming that both the Earth and Pluto are spherical, the diameter of Pluto is:

    F. 0.729 • the radius of Earth.
    G. 0.9 • the radius of Earth.
    H. 1.8 • the radius of Earth.
    J. 2.7 • the radius of Earth.

11. How many meters separate the orbits of the farthest apart planetary neighbors?

    A. 40 • Earth's orbital radius
    B. 11 • Earth's orbital radius
    C. 10 • Earth's orbital radius
    D. 9 • Earth's orbital radius

Passage III

Four groups of 1,000 men each were placed on strict diets that contained different intakes of cholesterol. The men stayed on the diet for 40 years, and their history of illness over that time is recorded below.

	Death rate, standardized/1,000			
		Men taking in a daily average of		
Illness	No cholesterol	0–5 grams	6–20 grams	20+ grams
Cancer				
Colon	0.01	0.03	0.04	0.02
Prostate	2.02	0.06	1.03	4.01
Lung	0.03	0.06	0.40	0.20
Coronary				
Thrombosis	5.02	1.01	4.00	10.05
Arrest	6.00	0.98	5.09	11.00
Cardiovascular	5.96	0.65	4.97	9.08
Cerebral Clot	4.01	0.02	0.50	4.01
Depression	5.01	0.30	0.30	0.30

12. Which of the following statements is best supported by the data?

    F. A man ingesting no cholesterol is approximately twice as likely to die of prostate cancer as a man ingesting 10 grams per day.
    G. Any ingestion of cholesterol decreases the risk of dying from all three forms of cancer listed here.
    H. Ingestion of cholesterol seems unrelated to the probability of coronary disease.
    J. Cerebral clots are the most prevalent form of death among the group consuming the most cholesterol.

13. What might one conclude about the relationship between cholesterol ingestion and depression based on the information above?

    A. Cholesterol causes depression.
    B. Ingestion of cholesterol has no effect on the occurrence of depression.
    C. Small amounts of cholesterol are most effective in combating depression.
    D. Large and small amounts of cholesterol are equally effective in reducing the depression death rate.

14. For which of the following diseases does the highest cholesterol diet increase the probability of death most, compared relatively to the non-cholesterol diets?

    F. Cerebral clots
    G. Coronary arrest
    H. Cardiovascular disease
    J. Coronary thrombosis

15. For which of the following groups of diseases does a daily intake of 0-5 grams of cholesterol reduce the probability of death?

    A. Cerebral clot, coronary thrombosis, and lung cancer
    B. Cerebral clot, depression, and colon cancer
    C. Depression, coronary arrest, and prostate cancer
    D. Depression, coronary thrombosis, and colon cancer

16. What might be involved in determining a standardized death rate for men?

    F. Ignoring deaths that do not conform to the average results
    G. Adjusting death rates according to discrepancies in age
    H. Assuming that the natural death rate is 0 deaths per 1,000 men
    J. Comparing data with a similar experiment involving women

GO ON TO THE NEXT PAGE

Passage IV

The resistance (R) of a material is directly proportional to the resistivity (r) of the material, resistivity is measured in ohm-meters. The voltage (V, measured in volts) in a circuit is directly proportional to both the resistance (R, measured in ohms) and the current (I, measured in amperes). Resistors in series act as one resistor according to the formula:

$$R_s = R_1 + R_2 + R_3 + \ldots$$

and resistors in parallel act as one resistor according to the formula:

$$\frac{1}{R_p} = \frac{1}{R_1} + \frac{1}{R_2} + \frac{1}{R_3} + \ldots$$

The resistivities of several materials are listed below.

Substance	Resistivity, r (ohm-meters)
Aluminum	$2.63 \cdot 10^{-8}$
Copper	$1.72 \cdot 10^{-8}$
Germanium	$6.00 \cdot 10^{-1}$
Silicon	$2.30 \cdot 10^{3}$
Silver	$1.47 \cdot 10^{-8}$
Sulfur	$1.00 \cdot 10^{15}$

17. According to the information provided, the best formula for the voltage in a circuit, where voltage is V, current is I, and resistance is R is:

    A. $V = \frac{I}{R}$.
    B. $V = I + R$.
    C. $V = IR$.
    D. $V = I - R$.

18. According to the information provided, how would the voltage in a circuit with a silver resistor compare to the voltage in a circuit with a germanium resistor of the same size? (Current is the same in both circuits.)

    F. The voltage in the silver circuit would be greater.
    G. The voltage in the germanium circuit would be greater.
    H. The voltage would be the same in both circuits.
    J. Cannot be determined from the given information

19. Two resistors with $R = 2$ are placed in series. How does the voltage in the circuit compare with the voltage in a circuit with only one resistor, $R = 2$? (Assume current remains constant.)

    A. The voltage is doubled.
    B. The voltage is halved.
    C. The voltage is the same.
    D. The voltage is zero.

20. A resistor with $R = 4$ is put in parallel with an identical resistor, $R = 4$. What is R_p?

    F. 0
    G. $\frac{1}{2}$
    H. 1
    J. 2

21. Power is defined as $P = I^2 R$. If R is a constant, then power would increase —— with an increase in the current. (Fill in the blank space with the best answer choice.)

    A. logarithmically
    B. directly
    C. exponentially
    D. inversely

22. In order to keep the current in a circuit constant, if one increases the voltage, one must:

    F. lengthen the circuit.
    G. shorten the circuit.
    H. decrease the resistance.
    J. increase the resistance.

Passage V

In order to discover the steps by which a chemical reaction occurs, the dependence of the initial rate of reaction on the concentration of the reactants is determined. Three experiments exploring the mechanism of a reaction are presented below.

Experiment 1: Compound A is injected into a rapidly stirred solution of B in hexamethyl phosphoramide. As A and B react, they form a compound that has a characteristic absorption at 520 nanometers. The concentration of product, and therefore the rate of reaction, can be calculated by measuring the strength of the absorption. Results are presented below:

Trial	Concentration A	Concentration B	Rate
1	4	4	60
2	2	2	30
3	4	2	30
4	4	8	120

Experiment 2: Compound A is injected into a rapidly mixed solution of B in carbon tetrachloride. The product of the reaction is identical to the product in Experiment 1. The course of the reaction is followed by spectrophotometric methods as in Experiment 1.

Trial	Concentration A	Concentration B	Rate
1	3	3	27
2	6	6	108
3	6	3	54
4	12	6	216

Experiment 3: Compound A is injected in a swirling solution of B in a 1:1-by-volume mixture of carbon tetrachloride and hexamethyl phosphoramide. The formation of product, as before, is followed by spectrophotometry.

Trial	Concentration A	Concentration B	Rate
1	9	9	54
2	9	4.5	27
3	4	4.5	18
4	4	9	36

23. Which of the following statements best describes the effect of Concentration A on the rate of reaction in Experiment 1?

   A. Rate increases with increasing A.
   B. Rate increases by the square of A's concentration.
   C. Rate increases by the square root of A's concentration.
   D. Rate is independent of A's concentration.

24. Which of the following statements best describes the effect of Concentration A on the rate of reaction in Experiment 2?

   F. Rate increases with increasing A.
   G. Rate increases by the square of A's concentration.
   H. Rate increases by the square root of A's concentration.
   J. Rate is independent of A's concentration.

25. Which of the following statements best describes the effect of Concentration A on the rate in Experiment 3?

   A. Rate increases with increasing A.
   B. Rate increases by the square of A's concentration.
   C. Rate increases by the square root of A's concentration.
   D. Rate is independent of A's concentration.

26. What is the likeliest explanation for the results obtained in Experiment 3?

   F. A mechanism intermediates between the ones found in Experiments 1 and 2.
   G. Some of the molecules react by Experiment 1's mechanism, others by Experiment 2's mechanism.
   H. A different mechanism is responsible.
   J. There is an averaging of the mechanisms.

27. What is the best conclusion that can be drawn from this set of experiments?

   A. Rate is increased by changing solvents.
   B. Reactions may depend on solvent effects as well as on the nature of the reactants.
   C. Mechanisms can always be changed by use of an appropriate solvent.
   D. Reactions depend on solvent effects as well as on the nature of the reactants.

Passage VI

Acceleration is defined as the change in the velocity of an object divided by the length of time during which that change took place. Contrary to popular belief, Galileo did not base his conclusion of the acceleration of gravity on experiments done with cannonballs dropped from the Leaning Tower of Pisa. Instead, he used the motion of objects moving down an inclined plane to develop his theory. In the following sets of experiments, a student studies the motion of bodies on an inclined plane.

For all of the following experiments, time is measured in seconds, distance in meters, and velocity in meters per second. The distance (d) an object travels at a constant acceleration (a) in time (t), assuming it starts from rest, is given by the equation: $d = \frac{1}{2}at^2$.

Experiment 1: A student set up a smooth wooden board at an angle of 30° from horizontal. The board had a length of 10 meters. Using a stroboscope, the student was able to determine the position of a 100-gram steel ball that was rolled down the incline. Velocity was determined by means of a radar gun. The results are presented below:

Time	Distance (m)	Velocity (m/sec)
0	0	0
0.5	0.44	1.75
1.0	1.75	3.5
1.5	3.94	5.25
2.0	7.00	7.00

Experiment 2: The same 10-meter wooden board was used in Experiment 2. The angle used was again 30°. The object used this time was a 100-gram sled made of the same material as the ball in Experiment 1. The stroboscope and the radar gun were used to determine its position and velocity as it slid down the inclined plane. The results are presented below:

Time	Distance (m)	Velocity (m/sec)
0	0	0
0.5	1.13	2.45
1.0	2.45	4.90
1.5	5.51	7.35
2.0	9.80	9.80

Experiment 3: The same board at the same angle was used in the third experiment as in the previous two. In this experiment, a 100-gram box made of the same material as the ball and the sled was used. The same recording devices were used, and the results are presented below:

Time	Distance (m)	Velocity (m/sec)
0	0	0
1.0	0.33	0.66
2.0	1.31	1.32
3.0	2.97	1.98
4.0	5.28	2.64
5.0	8.25	3.30

Experiment 4: The board in the previous experiments was carefully oiled. Once again, the board was placed at an angle of 30° from horizontal. Each of the objects was then allowed to move down the inclined plane, and the time required to reach the bottom of the plane is recorded below:

Object	Time
sled	2.02
ball	2.39
box	4.08

28. Which object in the first three experiments has the greatest acceleration?

    F. Ball
    G. Sled
    H. Box
    J. Ball and sled are equal.

29. The acceleration of the ball relative to that of the sled is due to the ball's:

    A. rolling.
    B friction.
    C. rolling and friction.
    D. being the same mass as the sled, and therefore having the same acceleration.

30. The acceleration of the ball relative to that of the box is due to:

    F. the ball's rolling only.
    G. the ball's friction only.
    H. the ball's rolling and the box's friction.
    J. the ball's having the same mass as the box, and therefore having the same acceleration.

31. Based on these four experiments, the ratio of the acceleration of the ball to the acceleration of the sled is:

    A. 1.
    B. $\frac{5}{7}$.
    C. dependent on the amount of friction.
    D. dependent on time.

32. Based on these four experiments, the ratio of the acceleration of the ball to the acceleration of the box is:

    F. 1.
    G. $\frac{5}{7}$.
    H. dependent on the amount of friction.
    J. dependent on time.

Passage VII

What was the fate of Neanderthal man? Two differing views are presented below.

Scientist 1: Neanderthals were very similar to modern humans in appearance. It is true that Neanderthals were somewhat more muscular than modern humans and that the way the muscles seem to have been arranged on the skeleton was, in a few minor ways, different. This we are able to deduce from the places on the surviving bones that mark where the ligaments were once attached. For example, the neck and wrists of Neanderthals were far thicker than is natural to modern humans. Some of the facial structure was also different, especially the protrusion of the brow. But differences between the appearance of Neanderthals and modern humans have been exaggerated since they are based on the skeleton of one individual who was later discovered to have been suffering from severe arthritis. It is not unlikely that, because of the low population density and the nomadic lifestyle that spread the few individuals over ever-larger areas, Neanderthal and early modern humans interbred and eventually merged into one species. The notion that some sort of "war" broke out between these different species (or, more likely, subspecies) of humans is an attempt to look out of early human eyes with a modern perspective.

Scientist 2: Whenever two species compete for the same niche there is a conflict. In this conflict the loser either moves to a different niche or dies out. It is unusual for two species to interbreed. The difference between early modern humans and Neanderthals physically may not appear great to an anatomist, but to the average man on the street, or prehistoric man in the forest, the differences are not subtle. And it was these individuals, not the anatomists, who had to decide whether or not to mate. Even if early modern humans and Neanderthals did mate, the result—us—would look more like a mix of the two rather than like modern humans. Early modern humans and Neanderthals, because they were so close to each other physically, must have been deadly enemies. The population was thinly dispersed at that time because the resources available would not support a greater population density. There literally was not room enough on the planet for the two species. They could not combine because they were so different in appearance, so only one answer remained. We survived because we killed our cousin.

33. Underlying the hypothesis of Scientist 1 is the assumption that:

    A. early modern humans and Neanderthals did not compete for the same kinds of food.
    B. early modern humans and Neanderthals were genetically close.
    C. early modern humans and Neanderthals did not necessarily live in the same area.
    D. early modern humans and Neanderthals often fought.

34. Underlying the hypotheses of both scientists is the assumption that:

    F. early modern humans and Neanderthals understood the consequences of their actions.
    G. early modern humans and Neanderthals both lived in exactly the same type of environment.
    H. early modern humans and Neanderthals both lived in the same geographical regions.
    J. early modern humans were more intelligent than Neanderthals.

35. If an isolated community of Neanderthals was discovered, whose hypothesis would be more damaged?

    A. Scientist 1's because his theory does not allow for such a community to survive
    B. Scientist 2's because the descendants of early modern humans inhabit all the Earth and therefore there should be no community of Neanderthals
    C. Both hypotheses are disproved.
    D. Neither hypothesis is affected.

36. Which of the following, if true, would most support the hypothesis of Scientist 2?

    F. The camps of early modern humans are often close to the camps of Neanderthals.
    G. The camps of early modern humans are never close to Neanderthal camps.
    H. Bones of Neanderthals and early modern humans are often found near each other.
    J. Chipped Neanderthal bones are found with early modern human weapons.

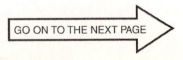

37. The fact that lions and tigers fight when brought together even though they can be interbred supports which hypothesis to the greater extent?

   A. Scientist 1's hypothesis, because it proves two species can interbreed
   B. Scientist 1's hypothesis, because two species still exist that share the same niche
   C. Scientist 2's hypothesis, because it suggests that two species that can interbreed may not do so under natural conditions
   D. Scientist 2's hypothesis, because lions and tigers fight when brought together

38. According to the hypothesis of Scientist 2, what should be the result of interbreeding lions and tigers?

   F. The offspring should be infertile.
   G. The offspring will resemble one parent only.
   H. The offspring will possess a mixture of traits.
   J. Scientist 2's hypothesis makes no conjectures on the point because lions and tigers would not interbreed.

39. What other assumption do both Scientist 1 and Scientist 2 make about Neanderthals and early modern humans?

   A. That early modern humans were directly involved in the disappearance of Neanderthals
   B. That early modern humans were the more intelligent of the two
   C. That Neanderthals differed little from early modern humans
   D. That early modern humans only inhabited regions that were hospitable for Neanderthals

40. If a burial site containing over one hundred early modern humans and Neanderthal remains was discovered, and if two Neanderthal skeletons were found with early modern human spearpoints in them, which hypothesis would be the most strengthened?

   F. Scientist 1's hypothesis, because spearpoints need not have been what killed the two Neanderthals
   G. Scientist 2's hypothesis, because two Neanderthals were killed by early modern humans and no early modern humans were killed by Neanderthals
   H. Scientist 2's hypothesis, because the spearpoints prove that the early modern humans had more developed weapons
   J. Scientist 1's hypothesis, because only a couple of the individuals buried together died violently

STEP FIVE: FINAL EXAM, ASSESSMENT REPORT, AND REVIEW

ACT • PLAN • EXPLORE
SCIENCE REASONING

STEP FIVE: FINAL EXAM, ASSESSMENT REPORT, AND REVIEW

CAMBRIDGE COURSE CONCEPT OUTLINE

AMERICA'S #1 STANDARDS-BASED SCHOOL IMPROVEMENT

Cambridge Course Concept Outline
STEP FIVE

I. **ACT • PLAN • EXPLORE DIAGNOSTIC POST-TEST PROGRESS REPORTS** (p. 173)

    A. **ACT • PLAN EXPLORE DIAGNOSTIC POST-TEST STUDENT PROGRESS REPORT** (p. 173)

    A. **ACT • PLAN EXPLORE DIAGNOSTIC POST-TEST INSTRUCTOR PROGRESS REPORT** (p. 175)

II. **ACT • PLAN • EXPLORE POST-TEST BUBBLE SHEET** (p. 177)

PROGRESS REPORTS

ACT • PLAN • EXPLORE
DIAGNOSTIC POST-TEST PROGRESS REPORT
(Student Copy)

DIRECTIONS: These progress reports are designed to help you make sense of your ACT, PLAN, or EXPLORE Science Reasoning Diagnostic Post-Test results. Complete the diagnostic post-test and record both the number and percentage of Science Reasoning problems answered correctly. Refer to your Cambridge Assessment Report when recording this information if your program has elected to use the Cambridge Assessment Service. Identify the date on which you completed the Science Reasoning section of the post-test, and list the numbers of any problems that you would like your instructor to review in class.

Transfer this information to the Instructor Copy, and then give that report to your instructor.

Name _____ Student ID _____ Date _____

DIAGNOSTIC POST-TEST
(Student Copy)

Test Section	Total # Possible	# Correct	% Correct	Date Completed	Problem #s to Review
ACT, PLAN, or EXPLORE SCIENCE REASONING					

Photocopying not allowed without Cambridge licensing agreement.

STEP FIVE

SCALE CONVERSION CHART
(Student Copy)

DIRECTIONS: This Scale Conversion Chart will help you translate the number of problems that you answered correctly into a scaled score. Record both the number and percentage of Science Reasoning problems that you answered correctly. Then, use the % Correct column to identify your raw score for this test. Find and record the raw score that corresponds to the scaled score that you earned on Table 1 in the back of your official, retired, test booklet.

Transfer this information to the Instructor Copy, and then give that report to your instructor.

DIAGNOSTIC POST-TEST SCORE CALCULATION				
	Total # Possible	# Correct	% Correct	Scale Score
SCIENCE REASONING Diagnostic Post-Test				

% CORRECT CHART							
Raw Score	40 Questions Total	60 Questions Total	75 Questions Total	Raw Score	40 Questions Total	60 Questions Total	75 Questions Total
1	3%	2%	1%	39	98%	65%	52%
2	5%	3%	3%	40	100%	67%	53%
3	8%	5%	4%	41		68%	55%
4	10%	7%	5%	42		70%	56%
5	13%	8%	7%	43		72%	57%
6	15%	10%	8%	44		73%	59%
7	18%	12%	9%	45		75%	60%
8	20%	13%	11%	46		77%	61%
9	23%	15%	13%	47		78%	63%
10	25%	17%	14%	48		80%	64%
11	28%	18%	15%	49		82%	65%
12	30%	20%	17%	50		83%	67%
13	33%	22%	18%	51		85%	68%
14	35%	23%	19%	52		87%	69%
15	38%	25%	20%	53		88%	71%
16	40%	27%	21%	54		90%	72%
17	43%	28%	23%	55		92%	73%
18	45%	30%	24%	56		93%	75%
19	48%	32%	25%	57		95%	76%
20	50%	33%	27%	58		97%	77%
21	53%	35%	28%	59		98%	79%
22	55%	37%	29%	60		100%	80%
23	58%	38%	31%	61			81%
24	60%	40%	32%	62			83%
25	63%	42%	33%	63			84%
26	65%	43%	35%	64			85%
27	68%	45%	36%	65			87%
28	70%	47%	37%	66			88%
29	73%	48%	39%	67			89%
30	75%	50%	40%	68			91%
31	78%	52%	41%	69			92%
32	80%	53%	43%	70			93%
33	83%	55%	44%	71			95%
34	85%	57%	45%	72			96%
35	88%	58%	47%	73			97%
36	90%	60%	48%	74			99%
37	93%	62%	49%	75			100%
38	95%	63%	51%				

PROGRESS REPORTS

ACT • PLAN • EXPLORE
DIAGNOSTIC POST-TEST PROGRESS REPORT
(Instructor Copy)

DIRECTIONS: Transfer the information from your Student Copy to the Instructor Copy below. Leave the last two bolded columns blank. Your instructor will use them to evaluate your progress. When finished, give these reports to your instructor.

Student Name _____ Student ID _____ Date _____

DIAGNOSTIC POST-TEST
(Instructor Copy)

Test Section	Total # Possible	# Correct	% Correct	Date Completed	Problem #s to Review	Instructor Skill Evaluation	
						Review Needed? (Y or N)	Section and Problem Numbers Assigned
ACT, PLAN, or EXPLORE SCIENCE REASONING							

 STEP FIVE

SCALE CONVERSION CHART
(Instructor Copy)

DIRECTIONS: Transfer the information from your Student Copy to the Instructor Copy below. When finished, give these reports to your instructor.

DIAGNOSTIC POST-TEST SCORE CALCULATION				
	Total # Possible	# Correct	% Correct	Scale Score
SCIENCE REASONING Diagnostic Post-Test				

% CORRECT CHART							
Raw Score	40 Questions Total	60 Questions Total	75 Questions Total	Raw Score	40 Questions Total	60 Questions Total	75 Questions Total
1	3%	2%	1%	39	98%	65%	52%
2	5%	3%	3%	40	100%	67%	53%
3	8%	5%	4%	41		68%	55%
4	10%	7%	5%	42		70%	56%
5	13%	8%	7%	43		72%	57%
6	15%	10%	8%	44		73%	59%
7	18%	12%	9%	45		75%	60%
8	20%	13%	11%	46		77%	61%
9	23%	15%	13%	47		78%	63%
10	25%	17%	14%	48		80%	64%
11	28%	18%	15%	49		82%	65%
12	30%	20%	17%	50		83%	67%
13	33%	22%	18%	51		85%	68%
14	35%	23%	19%	52		87%	69%
15	38%	25%	20%	53		88%	71%
16	40%	27%	21%	54		90%	72%
17	43%	28%	23%	55		92%	73%
18	45%	30%	24%	56		93%	75%
19	48%	32%	25%	57		95%	76%
20	50%	33%	27%	58		97%	77%
21	53%	35%	28%	59		98%	79%
22	55%	37%	29%	60		100%	80%
23	58%	38%	31%	61			81%
24	60%	40%	32%	62			83%
25	63%	42%	33%	63			84%
26	65%	43%	35%	64			85%
27	68%	45%	36%	65			87%
28	70%	47%	37%	66			88%
29	73%	48%	39%	67			89%
30	75%	50%	40%	68			91%
31	78%	52%	41%	69			92%
32	80%	53%	43%	70			93%
33	83%	55%	44%	71			95%
34	85%	57%	45%	72			96%
35	88%	58%	47%	73			97%
36	90%	60%	48%	74			99%
37	93%	62%	49%	75			100%
38	95%	63%	51%				

ACT • PLAN • EXPLORE Post-Test Bubble Sheet

Name _____ Student ID Number _____

Date _____ Instructor _____ Course/Session Number _____

TEST 1—ENGLISH

(Answer bubbles for questions 1–75, options A B C D / F G H J)

TEST 2—MATHEMATICS

(Answer bubbles for questions 1–60, options A B C D E / F G H J K)

TEST 3—READING

(Answer bubbles for questions 1–40, options A B C D / F G H J)

TEST 4—SCIENCE REASONING

(Answer bubbles for questions 1–40, options A B C D / F G H J)

STEP SIX: PERSONAL STUDY PLAN

ACT • PLAN • EXPLORE
SCIENCE REASONING

STEP SIX: PERSONAL STUDY PLAN

AMERICA'S #1 STANDARDS-BASED SCHOOL IMPROVEMENT

Cambridge Course Concept Outline
STEP SIX

I. **ACT • PLAN • EXPLORE SCIENCE REASONING STEP SIX PROGRESS REPORTS** (p. 185)

    A. ACT • PLAN EXPLORE SCIENCE REASONING STEP SIX STUDENT PROGRESS REPORT (p. 185)

    B. ACT • PLAN EXPLORE SCIENCE REASONING STEP SIX INSTUCTOR PROGRESS REPORT (p. 187)

II. **ACT • PLAN • EXPLORE ENGLISH STEP SIX PROGRESS REPORTS** (p. 189)

    A. ACT • PLAN EXPLORE ENGLISH STEP SIX STUDENT PROGRESS REPORT (p. 189)

    B. ACT • PLAN EXPLORE ENGLISH STEP SIX INSTUCTOR PROGRESS REPORT (p. 191)

III. **ACT • PLAN • EXPLORE MATHEMATICS STEP SIX PROGRESS REPORTS** (p. 193)

    A. ACT • PLAN EXPLORE MATHEMATICS STEP SIX STUDENT PROGRESS REPORT (p. 193)

    B. ACT • PLAN EXPLORE MATHEMATICS STEP SIX INSTUCTOR PROGRESS REPORT (p. 195)

IV. **ACT • PLAN • EXPLORE READING STEP SIX PROGRESS REPORTS** (p. 197)

    A. ACT • PLAN EXPLORE READING STEP SIX STUDENT PROGRESS REPORT (p. 197)

    B. ACT • PLAN EXPLORE READING STEP SIX INSTUCTOR PROGRESS REPORT (p. 199)

PROGRESS REPORTS

ACT • PLAN • EXPLORE SCIENCE REASONING
STEP SIX PROGRESS REPORT
(Student Copy)

DIRECTIONS: This progress report is designed to help you assess your overall course progress, evaluate your test-taking strengths and weaknesses, and create a study plan that will help you maximize your test score.

Fill this report out with the help of your instructor. Refer to your Steps One through Five Progress Reports to assess how you performed on each ACT • PLAN • EXPLORE Science Reasoning problem-type. Begin filling out this Progress Report by ranking your performance throughout the course by subject area. Rank your weakest area as number 1. Then, with your instructor, identify specific skills and strategies to focus on within each area (*e.g.*, pacing and guessing). Finally, work together to identify problems in the textbook, on the CD-ROM, or in your web course that will allow you to hone the skills necessary to improve in your weakest areas.

Work through as many of the additional review problems as possible before your test in order to perform to your potential on the actual exam.

Transfer this information to the Instructor Copy, and then give that report to your instructor.

Name _____ Student ID _____ Date _____

STUDY PLAN
(Student Copy)

Problem-Type	*Rank (1 = Weakest)*	*Strategies and Skills on Which to Focus*	*Additional Review Sections and Problem Numbers*
Data Representation Passages			
Research Summary Passages			
Conflicting Viewpoints Passages			

Photocopying not allowed without Cambridge licensing agreement.

PROGRESS REPORTS

ACT • PLAN • EXPLORE SCIENCE REASONING
STEP SIX PROGRESS REPORT
(Instructor Copy)

DIRECTIONS: Transfer the information from your Student Copy to the Instructor Copy below. When finished, give these reports to your instructor.

Student Name _____ Student ID _____ Date _____

STUDY PLAN
(Instructor Copy)

Problem-Type	Rank (1 = Weakest)	Strategies and Skills on Which to Focus	Additional Review Sections and Problem Numbers
Data Representation Passages			
Research Summary Passage			
Conflicting Viewpoints			

Photocopying not allowed without Cambridge licensing agreement.

PROGRESS REPORTS

ACT • PLAN • EXPLORE ENGLISH
STEP SIX PROGRESS REPORT
(Student Copy)

DIRECTIONS: This progress report is designed to help you assess your overall course progress, evaluate your test-taking strengths and weaknesses, and create a study plan that will help you maximize your test score.

Fill this report out with the help of your instructor. Refer to your Steps One through Five Progress Reports to assess how you performed on each ACT • PLAN • EXPLORE English problem-type. Begin filling out this Progress Report by ranking your performance throughout the course by subject area. Rank your weakest area as number 1. Then, with your instructor, identify specific skills and strategies to focus on within each area (*e.g.*, pacing and guessing). Finally, work together to identify problems in the textbook, on the CD-ROM, or in your web course that will allow you to hone the skills necessary to improve in your weakest areas.

Work through as many of the additional review problems as possible before your test in order to perform to your potential on the actual exam.

Transfer this information to the Instructor Copy, and then give that report to your instructor.

Name _____ Student ID _____ Date _____

STUDY PLAN
(Student Copy)

Problem-Type	Rank (1 = Weakest)	Strategies and Skills on Which to Focus	Additional Review Sections and Problem Numbers
Parts of Speech			
Common Grammatical Errors			
Analyzing Sentence Structure			
Problems of Logical Expression			
Idioms and Clarity of Expression			
Punctuation			
Capitalization and Spelling			

Photocopying not allowed without Cambridge licensing agreement.

PROGRESS REPORTS

ACT • PLAN • EXPLORE ENGLISH
STEP SIX PROGRESS REPORT
(Instructor Copy)

DIRECTIONS: Transfer the information from your Student Copy to the Instructor Copy below. When finished, give these reports to your instructor.

Student Name _____ Student ID _____ Date _____

STUDY PLAN
(Instructor Copy)

Problem-Type	*Rank (1 = Weakest)*	*Strategies and Skills on Which to Focus*	*Additional Review Sections and Problem Numbers*
Parts of Speech			
Common Grammatical Errors			
Analyzing Sentence Structure			
Problems of Logical Expression			
Idioms and Clarity of Expression			
Punctuation			
Capitalization and Spelling			

Photocopying not allowed without Cambridge licensing agreement.

PROGRESS REPORTS

ACT • PLAN • EXPLORE MATHEMATICS
STEP SIX PROGRESS REPORT
(Student Copy)

DIRECTIONS: This progress report is designed to help you assess your overall course progress, evaluate your test-taking strengths and weaknesses, and create a study plan that will help you maximize your test score.

Fill this report out with the help of your instructor. Refer to your Steps One through Five Progress Reports to assess how you performed on each ACT • PLAN • EXPLORE Mathematics problem-type. Begin filling out this Progress Report by ranking your performance throughout the course by subject area. Rank your weakest area as number 1. Then, with your instructor, identify specific skills and strategies to focus on within each area (*e.g.*, pacing and guessing). Finally, work together to identify problems in the textbook, on the CD-ROM, or in your web course that will allow you to hone the skills necessary to improve in your weakest areas.

Work through as many of the additional review problems as possible before your test in order to perform to your potential on the actual exam.

Transfer this information to the Instructor Copy, and then give that report to your instructor.

Name _____ Student ID _____ Date _____

STUDY PLAN
(Student Copy)

Problem-Type	*Rank (1 = Weakest)*	*Strategies and Skills on Which to Focus*	*Additional Review Sections and Problem Numbers*
Arithmetic			
Algebra			
Common Equations			
Geometry			
Trigonometry			

Photocopying not allowed without Cambridge licensing agreement.

ACT • PLAN • EXPLORE MATHEMATICS
STEP SIX PROGRESS REPORT
(Instructor Copy)

DIRECTIONS: Transfer the information from your Student Copy to the Instructor Copy below. When finished, give these reports to your instructor.

Student Name _____ Student ID _____ Date _____

STUDY PLAN
(Instructor Copy)

Problem-Type	Rank (1 = Weakest)	Strategies and Skills on Which to Focus	Additional Review Sections and Problem Numbers
Arithmetic			
Algebra			
Common Equations			
Geometry			
Trigonometry			

PROGRESS REPORTS

ACT • PLAN • EXPLORE READING
STEP SIX PROGRESS REPORT
(Student Copy)

DIRECTIONS: This progress report is designed to help you assess your overall course progress, evaluate your test-taking strengths and weaknesses, and create a study plan that will help you maximize your test score.

Fill this report out with the help of your instructor. Refer to your Steps One through Five Progress Reports to assess how you performed on each ACT • PLAN • EXPLORE Reading problem-type. Begin filling out this Progress Report by ranking your performance throughout the course by subject area. Rank your weakest area as number 1. Then, with your instructor, identify specific skills and strategies to focus on within each area (*e.g.*, pacing and guessing). Finally, work together to identify problems in the textbook, on the CD-ROM, or in your web course that will allow you to hone the skills necessary to improve in your weakest areas.

Work through as many of the additional review problems as possible before your test in order to perform to your potential on the actual exam.

Transfer this information to the Instructor Copy, and then give that report to your instructor.

Name _____ Student ID _____ Date _____

STUDY PLAN
(Student Copy)

Problem-Type	*Rank (1 = Weakest)*	*Strategies and Skills on Which to Focus*	*Additional Review Sections and Problem Numbers*
Social Science			
Natural Science			
Prose Fiction			
Humanities			

PROGRESS REPORTS

ACT • PLAN • EXPLORE READING
STEP SIX PROGRESS REPORT
(Instructor Copy)

DIRECTIONS: Transfer the information from your Student Copy to the Instructor Copy below. When finished, give these reports to your instructor.

Student Name _____ Student ID _____ Date _____

STUDY PLAN
(Instructor Copy)

Problem-Type	Rank (1 = Weakest)	Strategies and Skills on Which to Focus	Additional Review Sections and Problem Numbers
Social Science			
Natural Science			
Prose Fiction			
Humanities			

Photocopying not allowed without Cambridge licensing agreement.

ANSWERS AND EXPLANATIONS

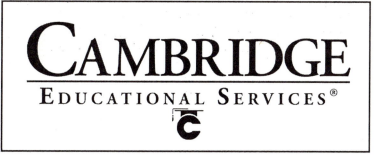

ACT • PLAN • EXPLORE SCIENCE REASONING

ANSWERS AND EXPLANATIONS

ANSWERS AND EXPLANATIONS

STEP TWO: SCIENCE SKILLS REVIEW

EXERCISE 1—BASICS OF EXPERIMENTAL DESIGN (p. 35)

1. The purpose of the experiment is to determine the effect of temperature on the heart rate of frogs.

2. The independent variable is temperature. (The experimenter determined the temperature before the experiment started.)

3. The dependent variable is heart rate.

4. When the temperature is increased, then the heart rate of the frogs will decrease.

5. The controlled variables are size, type, age, and number of frogs, as well as container size and amount of light.

6. The control group is Group C. (Group C refers to the frogs in the container that is approximately the same temperature as the enclosure from which the frogs were removed).

7. The experimental groups are Groups A, B, and D.

EXERCISE 2—DATA ORGANIZATION IN CONTROLLED EXPERIMENTS (p. 40)

1. The independent variable is the amount of time (in hours) over which the experiment was conducted. (The experimenter determined the amount of time before the experiment was started.)

2. The dependent variable is the percentage of carbohydrate digested. (In the data table, the independent variable was positioned in the first column and the dependent variable in the second column. The specific variations in the amount of time and the percentage of carbohydrates digested are positioned in the rows according to the increase in time.)

3. The independent variable is on the horizontal axis.

4. The dependent variable is on the vertical axis.

5. The slope of the line indicates that generally as the amount of time increases, the percentage of carbohydrates digested increases.

6. The correct answer is (C). The slope of the graph is greatest during the four hours between the eighth hour and the twelfth hour, so the greatest amount of carbohydrate digestion occurred during this period.

7. The independent variable is the source of salt.

8. The dependent variable is the percentage of salt.

9. The mammal with a percentage of salt in its urine closest to the percentage of salt in seawater is the human.

EXERCISE 3—PRESENTATION OF CONFLICTING VIEWPOINTS (p. 43)

1. The dependent variable (the problem) is the discovery of a dead woman.

2. The conflicting viewpoint is whether the death was a homicide or a suicide.

3. The independent variable causing the conflict is the lack of evidence indicating who shot the gun.

4.

Data	More Consistent with Detective I	More Consistent with Detective II	Equally Consistent with Both Detectives I and II
Gun Owned by Woman		✓	
Bloody Pillow			✓
Bruise on Head	✓		
Firecracker-Like Noise			✓
No Forced Entry			✓
Locked Door		✓	
No Suicide Note	✓		
Divorced Victim	✓		
Despondent Victim		✓	

Answers and Explanations

EXERCISE 4—SCIENCE REASONING PASSAGES (p. 44)

1. C	6. J	11. C	16. F	21. B
2. G	7. A	12. F	17. A	22. H
3. D	8. J	13. C	18. J	23. D
4. G	9. A	14. H	19. C	24. F
5. A	10. H	15. B	20. G	

STEP THREE: PROBLEM-SOLVING, CONCEPTS, AND STRATEGIES

SECTION ONE—SCIENCE REASONING REVIEW (p. 61)

1. B	10. H	19. B	28. J	37. D	46. H
2. F	11. A	20. F	29. B	38. F	47. D
3. C	12. H	21. C	30. G	39. B	48. H
4. G	13. D	22. F	31. C	40. H	49. D
5. C	14. F	23. D	32. H	41. C	50. G
6. H	15. C	24. G	33. D	42. G	51. C
7. D	16. F	25. B	34. F	43. A	52. F
8. H	17. D	26. F	35. C	44. J	53. D
9. C	18. J	27. B	36. G	45. D	54. F

SECTION TWO—SCIENCE REASONING PROBLEM-SOLVING (p. 76)

1. D	14. J	27. B	40. J	53. C	66. G
2. F	15. C	28. H	41. B	54. F	67. B
3. B	16. H	29. B	42. H	55. B	68. F
4. G	17. D	30. G	43. C	56. H	69. D
5. C	18. G	31. D	44. G	57. D	70. F
6. G	19. C	32. F	45. B	58. F	71. C
7. B	20. H	33. B	46. F	59. C	72. G
8. G	21. A	34. H	47. B	60. H	73. C
9. C	22. F	35. B	48. G	61. D	74. F
10. F	23. A	36. G	49. C	62. G	75. D
11. B	24. H	37. C	50. H	63. B	76. G
12. H	25. D	38. H	51. D	64. J	77. C
13. C	26. F	39. C	52. J	65. B	78. J

SECTION THREE—SCIENCE REASONING QUIZZES (p. 94)

QUIZ I

1. D	3. D	5. C	7. B	9. A
2. J	4. H	6. J	8. H	10. G

QUIZ II

1. A	3. A	5. C	7. D	9. C
2. F	4. J	6. H	8. F	10. G

QUIZ III

1. C	3. C	5. A	7. A	9. B	11. C
2. G	4. H	6. F	8. H	10. G	

ANSWERS AND EXPLANATIONS

STEP FOUR: PRACTICE TEST REINFORCEMENT

PRACTICE TEST I ANSWER KEY (p. 125)

DIRECTIONS: The following grid is used to score the practice test by question type. For each *correct* answer, check the corresponding unshaded box. Then, total the number of checkmarks for each of the two subject categories (UM, RH), and add these two totals in order to determine the raw score for each test.

TEST 4: SCIENCE REASONING

	B	C	P	ES			B	C	P	ES			B	C	P	ES
1. A						16. J						28. G				
2. F						17. B						29. C				
3. B						18. J						30. G				
4. H						19. D						31. D				
5. C						20. F						32. F				
6. J						21. C						33. A				
7. B						22. F						34. H				
8. H						23. B						35. B				
9. D						24. J						36. J				
10. F						25. C						37. C				
11. C						26. F						38. G				
12. H						27. D						39. D				
13. D												40. F				
14. G																
15. C																

Biology (B): ___/17 Earth Science (ES): ___/5

Chemistry (C): ___/12 Science Reasoning Raw Score (B + C + P + ES): ___/40

Physics (P): ___/6

PRACTICE TEST I EXPLANATORY ANSWERS (p. 125)

1. **(A)** All three of the tabulated properties generally increase with the number of carbons.

2. **(F)** The change from methane (-162° C) to ethane (-89° C) is greatest (73° C increase).

3. **(B)** This property can be seen by looking at propane (3 carbons: -188° C) to butane (4 carbons: -138° C), pentane (5 carbons: -130° C) to hexane (6 carbons: -95° C), *etc.*

4. **(H)** Only boiling points and number of carbons increase without exception.

5. **(C)** Pentane (0.56) to hexane (0.66) is an increase of 0.10 ($\frac{0.10}{0.56}$ = 18%).

6. **(J)** Momentum equals mass multiplied by velocity. Therefore, the momentum is:

    2 kilograms • 4 $\frac{m}{sec}$.

7. **(B)** The momentums of the two masses are initially 8 and 0; afterward, the momentum of the combined mass is 7.98.

8. **(H)** Notice the negative sign on the final velocity for Object 1, as well as the note in the text about the meaning of negative velocity.

9. **(D)** Since no actual value is given in the phrase "far more massive," it is unlikely that an explicit calculation is needed. To be successful, a reader needs to visualize a collision of a very light object with a massive one; the large one will not budge.

10. **(F)** The lighter object would recoil even faster than the observed -1.71 m/sec.

11. **(C)** Using the formula given, initial kinetic energy is found to be 16.0; the final kinetic energy has decreased to about 4.5.

12. **(H)** An increase in temperature influences flowering, while a decrease in temperature is one factor that causes leaf drop-off.

13. **(D)** The table shows that plant growth occurs when Hormones 1 and 3 increase. Yet, even if these two hormones increase, a similar increase in either H_4 or H_5 will lead to no plant growth—H_4 and H_5 inhibit growth.

14. **(G)** The table shows various factors that influence each plant activity. Seed germination is influenced by only one factor (H_3), while flowering is influenced by four different factors (H_3 and H_5, day length, and temperature).

15. **(C)** Changing a houseplant's growing conditions from 12 hours of light per 12 hours of dark to constant light is an example of altering day length, which only affects flowering.

16. **(J)** H_2 only affects flower drop-off, fruit drop-off, and leaf drop-off. For each of these activities, H_1 must also play a role (as H_2 increases, H_1 decreases).

17. **(B)** The only way the bag can gain weight between weighings is if additional fluid has moved inside. In this case, water moved inside (by osmosis) faster than it moved out.

18. **(J)** The fluid compartment (bag or beaker) that initially has only water (no red dye) never gets red. This indicates that the red dye is not free to pass across the bag's "membrane."

19. **(D)** In Experiment 2, the bag has gained 10 grams after only 10 minutes (water has entered the bag faster than in Experiment 1). By 20 minutes, more water will have entered and the bag should be even heavier.

20. **(F)** The experiments show that water will flow toward the compartment containing red dye. The more concentrated the red dye, the faster the flow of water.

21. **(C)** Water is free to flow into or out of the bag. Since there is no dye in the bag or the beaker, water will flow at an equal rate in both directions and the bag's weight should remain the same.

22. **(F)** Since salts are not able to enter or leave the cell, only water will move—in a direction that tends towards balanced concentrations. The water will flow toward the greater concentration of salt (from red blood cell to sea water), causing shrinkage of the cells.

23. **(B)** Magnesium is a positively charged mineral (Mg^{+2}). The soil that has the worst relative ability to hold such minerals is coarse sand.

24. **(J)** As particles get larger (from less than 2 micrometers to 200-2,000 micrometers), their relative ability to retain water decreases (from 1 to 4).

25. **(C)** Soils that are neither best nor worst at any ability cannot be ranked 1 or 4. The only soils that are never ranked 1 or 4 are silt (2-20 micrometers) and sand (20-200 micrometers). The total size range, therefore, is between 2-200 micrometers.

26. **(F)** Since loam is mostly clay, it primarily has small particles that hold minerals and water well. The larger silt and sand particles in loam are adequate at maintaining air spaces containing oxygen. None of the other predictions fit the data in the chart.

27. **(D)** Clay is best (relative ability: 1) at both holding positively charged minerals and retaining water.

28. **(G)** Concentrations of reactants, not products, determine rate in both theories.

29. **(C)** This question tests critical comprehension of the passage, and it requires an understanding of the relationship between the two theories.

30. **(G)** This question tests understanding of the relation of numbers of reactants in the overall equation to exponents in the rate law.

31. **(D)** The coefficients of the reactants determine their exponents in the rate law.

32. **(F)** This question tests comprehension of the differences between the theories.

33. **(A)** If the first stage is very slow and the second stage is much quicker, the overall rate is essentially that of the first stage.

Answers and Explanations

34. **(H)** If the sum of the rates of each stage always equaled the rate of the reaction taken as a whole, there would be no need to analyze each sub-reaction.

35. **(B)** Temperature range for a life function is the high temperature minus the low temperature. For both species and both humidity conditions, oviposition always has the narrowest range.

36. **(J)** For each life function, Species M achieved 90% success at the same low temperatures in moist or dry air. At high temperatures, however, dry air was detrimental (Under dry conditions, 90% success was not achieved at the same high temperatures as when conditions were moist!).

37. **(C)** Since dry conditions had no effect on Species D for mating, oviposition, or pupation, it is likely that dry conditions will have little effect on caterpillar survival in Species D as well. The temperature range would, therefore, be the same as observed at 100% relative humidity.

38. **(G)** Mating success in the light and in the dark should be compared at the same temperature. It should be a temperature at which both species can successfully mate. Otherwise, additional variables confuse the issue.

39. **(D)** Species M and Species D are both equally successful at low temperatures for pupation.

40. **(F)** (G) and (H) are not relevant to the question. (J) only refers to light conditions. (F) is a hypothesis supported by the results.

STEP FOUR

PRACTICE TEST II ANSWER KEY (p. 135)

DIRECTIONS: The following grid is used to score the practice test by question type. For each *correct* answer, check the corresponding unshaded box. Then, total the number of checkmarks for each of the two subject categories (UM, RH), and add these two totals in order to determine the raw score for each test.

TEST 4: SCIENCE REASONING

	B	C	P	ES			B	C	P	ES			B	C	P	ES
1. D						13. B						30. H				
2. F						14. J						31. D				
3. C						15. A						32. G				
4. J						16. G						33. C				
5. D						17. C						34. G				
6. H						18. J						35. D				
7. A						19. C						36. J				
8. G						20. F						37. B				
9. D						21. D						38. F				
10. F						22. H						39. B				
11. B						23. A						40. H				
12. H						24. G										
						25. C										
						26. H										
						27. B										
						28. G										
						29. B										

Biology (B): ____/11   Earth Science (ES): ____/6
Chemistry (C): ____/12   Science Reasoning Raw Score (B + C + P + ES): ____/40
Physics (P): ____/11

PRACTICE TEST II EXPLANATORY ANSWERS (p. 135)

1. **(D)** The radii increase (0.37, 1.35, 1.54, *etc.*) and the electronegativities decrease (2.20, 0.98, 0.93, *etc.*) as one goes down each column.

2. **(F)** It is essential to remember that the second number means electronegativity. For fluorine (F), it is 3.98.

3. **(C)** The bond length is the sum of the radii for each of the bonded atoms (1.10 + 0.99).

4. **(J)** Carbon and nitrogen have the smallest electronegativity difference, 0.49.

5. **(D)** Electronegativities increase steadily across each row and decrease steadily along each column, so the most widely separated elements have the most ionic bonds, or greatest ionic character.

6. **(H)** Several choices include the value 3.16, which is the electronegativity difference in RbF. Since Cs is below Rb, it may be expected to have an electronegativity below the value of 0.82, which is found for Rb, a prediction that leads to an electronegativity difference for CsF that is greater than 3.16.

7. **(A)** Venus is only 0.05 units smaller in diameter than Earth (0.95 Earth diameters).

8. **(G)** 1 A.U. equals 0.5 inches in the scale used in Experiment 2. The paper is only 14 inches long. Neptune's distance is 30 A.U. (30 • 0.5 = 15 inches) and would not fit on the paper (nor would Pluto, which is even farther away).

9. **(D)** As planets get farther from the Sun (A.U. column), some are larger than the Earth (Jupiter and Saturn have larger diameters), while others

are smaller than the Earth (Mars and Pluto have smaller diameters).

10. **(F)** If the asteroids are 2.8 A.U. away from the Sun, they would be found between Mars and Jupiter. Thus, an asteroid year is longer than that on Mars but shorter than that on Jupiter.

11. **(B)** If the Sun's diameter is 110 times greater than that of the Earth, its diameter would be 110 • 5 inches = 550 inches (Experiment 1 uses a scale where 1 Earth diameter = 5 inches).

12. **(H)** The relative mass information given in the question is very similar to the order of planets based on their relative diameters (Table 1: Earth diameters column).

13. **(B)** If carbon dioxide (CO_2) is the variable in question, all factors except carbon dioxide should remain fixed. Only then can the effects of various carbon dioxide levels be evaluated.

14. **(J)** The only difference between Experiments 1 and 2 is that the concentration of leaf extract (containing a mixture of pigments) was reduced in Experiment 2. Using the lower concentration of pigments, the rate of photosynthesis leveled off, suggesting that the amount was inadequate to maintain the previously observed increase in rate.

15. **(A)** The description of Experiment 3 states that wavelengths must be absorbed to maintain photosynthesis (which is measured by counting oxygen bubbles). The bubble counts (and therefore peak absorption) for Pigment A are at 450 and 650 nanometers. For Pigment B, peak count is between 500-575 nanometers.

16. **(G)** Since the reduced concentration of pigments in Experiment 2 led to a leveling off in bubble count, an increase in pigment concentration should lead to an increase in the rate of photosynthesis and an associated increase in bubbles.

17. **(C)** Proper interpretation of the graphs in Figures 1 and 2 reveals that at light intensity level of 4, 40-50 bubbles/minute are produced.

18. **(J)** Figure 3 shows that at 600 nm. (orange light), both Pigments A and B show very little absorption, as measured by the low oxygen bubble count. Since light must be absorbed to provide energy for photosynthesis, orange light would be least effective.

19. **(C)** The meters/minute scale increases from bottom to top. The highest point on the chart shows the fastest speed to be approximately 590-600 meters/minute.

20. **(F)** The lines represent the best-fitting slopes of points, which show how running speed has increased.

21. **(D)** In 1960, the ratio is based on 4 minutes/mile (1-mile run) to approximately 3.1 minutes/mile (440-yard dash).

22. **(H)** The speeds for the 2-mile run are all between 340-380 meters/minute. The gain in speed must be closest to the "30 meters/minute" choice.

23. **(A)** This problem, requiring the right-hand scale, asks for an extrapolation beyond the given data. The 880-yard line crosses the 1980 axis at approximately 3.5 minutes/mile.

24. **(G)** Temperature rises at an even rate during the time that the sample is heated.

25. **(C)** Experiment 1 starts above 0° C, whereas Experiment 2 starts below 0° C. In addition, the temperature in Experiment 2 stabilizes along the "x-axis" for a while.

26. **(H)** The passage states that "constant" amounts of heat were added "continuously" to samples over a "defined" period of time. Assuming that all of these given conditions remain unchanged, (F), (G), and (J) can be eliminated. Therefore, a process such as heat absorption is the best explanation for the flat part of the graph since it is not a given condition.

27. **(B)** Ice melts at 0° C. This is the temperature at which the graph temporarily levels off.

28. **(G)** The experiment utilized constant heating. Yet, temperature change was not constant.

29. **(B)** At the boiling point of water (100° C), there should be another flat section corresponding to the heat absorbed by the liquid in order to convert it to vapor.

30. **(H)** An examination of the diagram reveals that primary tissue layers and primary germ layers are names for the same developing parts. This information is part of the description of the gastrula stage.

31. **(D)** The diagram arrows show the changes that occur as each developmental stage follows the previous one. The greatest amount of differentiation in structure and function occurs during organogenesis as the primary germ layers in the gastrula become the many specialized systems, organs, and related structures of the organism.

32. **(G)** The arrows show that during organogenesis, the body's bones develop from the middle primary germ layer (mesoderm), not the innermost layer (endoderm).

33. **(C)** Structures (receptor cells) that contribute to visual abilities in the monkey would develop as parts of the eye, "a special sense organ." The arrows show that parts of the special sense organs arise from the ectoderm.

34. **(G)** The asterisk indicates that during cleavage the many new cells that form from the zygote and its materials do not grow. Thus, as the zygote's material is simply subdivided, the resulting cells must be extremely small.

35. **(D)** Theory 1 allows for all proportions of reactants.

36. **(J)** Theory 1 simply states that any proportion of reactants may mix. It does not explain the relation of the amounts of reactants to the amounts of product produced by the reaction.

37. **(B)** Theory 2 states that a certain proportion of reactants will react; if otherwise, one or another reactant will fail to react completely.

38. **(F)** Both reactants must be in the appropriate proportions to be used in the process of forming more product.

39. **(B)** This is the only response that provides a ratio of Fe to O that is different from the two ratios that proved successful in the problem.

40. **(H)** Theory 1 only states that products contain the original elements.

C ANSWERS AND EXPLANATIONS

PRACTICE TEST III ANSWER KEY (p. 145)

DIRECTIONS: The following grid is used to score the practice test by question type. For each *correct* answer, check the corresponding unshaded box. Then, total the number of checkmarks for each of the two subject categories (UM, RH), and add these two totals in order to determine the raw score for each test.

TEST 4: SCIENCE REASONING

	B	C	P	ES
1. C			✓	
2. H			✓	
3. A			✓	
4. H			✓	
5. C			✓	
6. J	✓			
7. A	✓			
8. H	✓			
9. C	✓			
10. G	✓			
11. A	✓			

	B	C	P	ES
12. G				✓
13. D				✓
14. H				✓
15. A				✓
16. F				✓
17. C				✓
18. G				✓
19. D	✓			
20. G	✓			
21. C	✓			
22. J	✓			
23. A	✓			
24. F	✓			

	B	C	P	ES
25. A				
26. J		✓		
27. D				
28. J				
29. C				
30. J				
31. C			✓	
32. J				
33. A				
34. H			✓	
35. C				
36. H	✓			
37. D	✓			
38. G	✓			
39. B	✓			
40. G	✓			

Biology (B): ___/17   Earth Science (ES): ___/7
Chemistry (C): ___/6   Science Reasoning Raw Score (B + C + P + ES): ___/40
Physics (P): ___/10

PRACTICE TEST III EXPLANATORY ANSWERS (p. 145)

1. **(C)** Generally, the Wright data show lower lift at a given angle than the Lilienthal data.

2. **(H)** The highest point on the graph is at 16 degrees (approximately 5.5 pounds/sq. ft.).

3. **(A)** By extending both lines to the 50° mark, the difference between them is clearly observed to be less than 1 pound/sq. ft.

4. **(H)** Count the crossing points of the two curves.

5. **(C)** The widest region is between 18° and 43°.

6. **(J)** Since plastic beads are not alive, they cannot possibly carry out cellular respiration. This control is designed to detect any atmospheric changes (in the laboratory) that may cause a change in gas volume inside the tubes.

7. **(A)** Oxygen in the air of the tube is consumed by the peas during cellular respiration (see summary equation).

8. **(H)** Without KOH to remove the carbon dioxide produced during cellular respiration, the same number of gas molecules ($6CO_2$) would always be added to the tube as gas molecules were being consumed in the tube ($6O_2$).

9. **(C)** Experiment 2 was conducted at a higher temperature than Experiment 1. The greater decrease in gas in the same time period (15 minutes) demonstrates a faster consumption of oxygen.

10. **(G)** If results are identical in light and dark (Experiments 1 and 2), then light/dark conditions are irrelevant to cellular respiration rates in the

experiment; only temperature conditions are important.

11. **(A)** Glucose must be consumed in order for cellular respiration to occur. Since cellular respiration did not occur at equal rates in Experiments 1 and 2, (A) is the only possible answer. Peas are seeds containing a supply of glucose.

12. **(G)** Scientist 1 believes that processes associated with sudden events in the past shaped the Earth, whereas Scientist 2 believes that the processes are continuing in the present.

13. **(D)** Mountains could not have formed only when land masses were raised at the beginnings of the Earth if recent fossils of sea creatures are found at mountain tops. This evidence suggests that the rocks were underwater relatively recently.

14. **(H)** Scientist 1 never refers to time or how old the Earth may be. Scientist 2 refers to "long" or "vast" periods of time.

15. **(A)** If the worldwide ocean precipitated granite first, it must be the lowest layer, with other precipitated materials covering it later.

16. **(F)** If the major rock types (three) formed when the worldwide ocean precipitated different materials on three occasions, no further types can be expected since this ocean no longer exists (possibly due to evaporation).

17. **(C)** Processes cannot be uniform from the beginning. Processes that formed the Earth at its origin must have differed from those that maintain and mold the Earth as an existing planet.

18. **(G)** Scientist 1 refers to three rock types forming during three separate precipitations. Regions of lava (with no present volcanoes), rivers presently continuing to cut their channels, and "related" fossils that could not have immigrated from other geographic areas are factors that support the views of Scientist 2.

19. **(D)** Ten individuals had their heart rates recorded every 10 minutes during a 30-minute experiment (three times). Therefore, 30 values were used to calculate the average heart rate for each of the experiments.

20. **(G)** Since Species B had an increase in heart rate when environmental temperature increased, it is the likely species to be poikilothermic (Species A's heart rate stayed about the same).

21. **(C)** Just by chance alone, any one individual might have an extremely high or extremely low heart rate. The larger the sample of individuals tested, the lower the chances of getting extreme average values.

22. **(J)** Since Species B (poikilothermic) had an increase in average heart rate when environmental temperature increased, a decrease in average heart rate is likely when temperatures drop. Species A should have approximately the same average heart rate at all three temperatures.

23. **(A)** At 22° C, Species A had an average heart rate of 150 beats/minute, while Species B averaged 100 beats/minute.

24. **(F)** The poikilothermic Species B should have an increase in body temperature in Experiment 2 (35° C conditions in the incubator compared to 22° C in Experiment 1). The homeothermic Species A should have no significant change in body temperature during the experiments.

25. **(A)** Each photon can promote an electron from level 1 to level 2 since the difference in energies is 0.60. (Note that the actual value of level 1 alone, which happens to be 0.60 also, does not determine the answer. Differences in energy are what matter.)

26. **(J)** There is no way to distinguish between the two emissions since each releases a photon of equal energy.

27. **(D)** Only the level 3 to level 1 emission has an energy difference of 0.92.

28. **(J)** Each electron can go from level 1 to any of 4 other levels, with each of the four transitions requiring a photon of a different energy.

29. **(C)** Since absorption of photons occurs first, then emission, electrons must be promoted (gaining the necessary energy from the absorbed photons), then emitted. Transitions between levels 3 and 4 have the necessary energies, namely 0.23.

30. **(J)** Although 2.07 is the absolute energy of level 5, there is no difference of energy levels anywhere

ANSWERS AND EXPLANATIONS

on the diagram that equals 2.07; hence, the photons will not be absorbed.

31. **(C)** Note how θ_1 and θ_2 are defined on the original drawing, then imagine how the diagram will change as the angles become smaller. (B) would be correct if the angles were defined as those between the ray and the horizontal, not vertical, axis.

32. **(J)** Only the last choice fits both experiments.

33. **(A)** This question simply requires interpretation of the meaning of the diagram.

34. **(H)** The beam of light only passes into the air for observation in Experiment 2.

35. **(C)** This response covers all elements of the three diagrams.

36. **(H)** The number of butterflies captured for marking is found under the heading: "# marked." Reading across the table for each size group, the "dark brown" category always has the fewest butterflies marked.

37. **(D)** By comparing the number of butterflies recaptured to the number marked, students can derive a proportion that represents how easy it is to recapture each type of butterfly. The proportion for small, white butterflies (30:35) is much higher than that for any of the other choices.

38. **(G)** An examination of the table shows that for all colors, as size increases the number of butterflies marked gets larger.

39. **(B)** A poisonous chemical will have adverse effects on the butterfly after marking (perhaps by killing or by preventing flight). The group with the lowest number (and proportion) of individuals recaptured in flight ($10:40 = 1:4 = \frac{1}{4}$ recaptured) is the group consisting of small, tan butterflies.

40. **(G)** For medium-sized butterflies, the proportion of individuals recaptured in each color is as follows: white (15:30 = 1:2), tan (20:40 = 1:2), and dark brown (10:20 = 1:2).

STEP FOUR

PRACTICE TEST IV ANSWER KEY (p. 157)

DIRECTIONS: The following grid is used to score the practice test by question type. For each *correct* answer, check the corresponding unshaded box. Then, total the number of checkmarks for each of the two subject categories (UM, RH), and add these two totals in order to determine the raw score for each test.

TEST 4: SCIENCE REASONING

	B	C	P	ES			B	C	P	ES			B	C	P	ES
1. B	☐					17. C			☐			28. G			☐	
2. H	☐					18. G			☐			29. A			☐	
3. D	☐					19. A			☐			30. H			☐	
4. J	☐					20. J			☐			31. B			☐	
5. B	☐					21. C			☐			32. H			☐	
6. G				☐		22. J			☐			33. B	☐			
7. A				☐		23. D		☐				34. H	☐			
8. J				☐		24. F		☐				35. D	☐			
9. B				☐		25. C		☐				36. J	☐			
10. H				☐		26. H		☐				37. C	☐			
11. B				☐		27. B		☐				38. H	☐			
12. F		☐										39. A	☐			
13. D		☐										40. G	☐			
14. J		☐									
15. C		☐									
16. G		☐									

Biology (B): ___/13
Chemistry (C): ___/10
Physics (P): ___/11
Earth Science (ES): ___/6
Science Reasoning Raw Score (B + C + P + ES): ___/40

PRACTICE TEST IV EXPLANATORY ANSWERS (p. 157)

1. **(B)** The sharpest sloping curve is for potassium nitrate (KNO_3).

2. **(H)** The sodium salts, NaCl and $NaNO_3$, have different solubilities, indicating that solubility depends on more than the nature of sodium. Thus, (F) and (G) must be incorrect. (J) is incorrect because it is not known whether the solubility curves for all sodium compounds have been given. (H) is correct because it takes into account the differences in solubilities of different sodium salts.

3. **(D)** The table gives data only for aqueous solutions, not alcoholic.

4. **(J)** Since the solubility curves intersect (at 71°C), the first material to leave solution depends on whether the maximum solubility is exceeded above or below the point of intersection.

5. **(B)** Soda goes flat as gas (carbon dioxide) leaves the liquid. The warmer the soda, the faster it goes flat. (A) shows the effect of pressure, not temperature, on solubility. (C) shows the solubility of a solid (sugar), which has nothing to do with the solubility characteristics of a gas. (D) deals with relative densities of gases and not with solubilities.

6. **(G)** Mercury's period of revolution equals 0.25 • period of Earth's revolution = 0.25 • 365.3 days ≈ 90 days. Mercury's period of rotation equals 60 • period of Earth's rotation = 60 • 1 day = 60 days. The ratio of revolution to rotation = $\frac{90}{60} = \frac{3}{2}$.

7. **(A)** Mercury's density equals that of the Earth. Density is mass divided by volume. Mercury's density = $\frac{\text{Mercury's mass}}{\text{Mercury's volume}} = \frac{0.58 \cdot \text{Earth's mass}}{0.58 \cdot \text{Earth's volume}} = \frac{\text{Earth's mass}}{\text{Earth's volume}}$ = Earth's density.

Answers and Explanations

8. **(J)** Rate is distance divided by time. Divide the average distance to the sun by the period of revolution to get the relative rate. The smallest relative rate is the slowest. In this specific case, the planet with the greatest relative period of revolution orbits the sun at the slowest rate.

9. **(B)** Gravity depends on both the distance between the centers of objects (and thereby the volume—assuming the planets are roughly spherical in shape) and on the mass of the objects. Compare Mars and Mercury to see the effect of volume (by considering their diameters). Mars is more massive, but the smaller size of Mercury gives it an equivalent surface gravity. Density, a ratio of mass and volume, is not enough because gravity depends on the amount of mass and the amount of distance, not their ratio.

10. **(H)** $\dfrac{\text{Pluto's volume}}{\text{Earth's volume}} = 0.729 \Rightarrow \dfrac{\frac{4}{3}\pi r^3_{\text{Pluto}}}{\frac{4}{3}\pi r^3_{\text{Earth}}} = 0.729 \Rightarrow$

    $\dfrac{r^3_{\text{Pluto}}}{r^3_{\text{Earth}}} = 0.729 \Rightarrow \dfrac{r_{\text{Pluto}}}{r_{\text{Earth}}} = \sqrt[3]{0.729} = 0.9$. Pluto's diameter $= 2 \cdot (0.9 \cdot \text{Earth's radius}) = 1.8$ times the Earth's radius.

11. **(B)** The neighbors that are farthest from each other are Uranus and Neptune. Relative distances to the sun are as follows:

    $\dfrac{\text{Mercury}}{0.4} < \dfrac{\text{Venus}}{0.7} < \dfrac{\text{Earth}}{1} < \dfrac{\text{Mars}}{1.5} < \dfrac{\text{Jupiter}}{5.3} < \dfrac{\text{Saturn}}{10} <$
    $\dfrac{\text{Uranus}}{19} < \dfrac{\text{Neptune}}{30} < \dfrac{\text{Pluto}}{40}$

    The largest difference $(30 - 19) = 11$.

12. **(F)** The death rate for the 6-20 gram/day cholesterol eater from prostate cancer is 1.03, while that for a non-cholesterol eater is 2.02. Thus, (F) is correct. (G) contradicts the data for colon cancer; (H) ignores the direct relationship between coronary deaths and cholesterol intake; and cardiac arrest is a more common form of death than cerebral clots for the 20+ eaters.

13. **(D)** The death rate for all three groups of cholesterol-eaters from depression is 0.30. This number is lower than for non-cholesterol-eaters, so (A) and (B) are both wrong. According to the data, large amounts of cholesterol are just as effective in combating depression as small amounts, so (C) is incorrect.

14. **(J)** Although the 20+ diet increases coronary arrest to the highest absolute death rate, the percentage increase is less than 100% (from 6.00 to 11.00). The percentage increase for coronary thrombosis is greater than 100% (from 5.02 to 10.05).

15. **(C)** (C) is the only group in which low intake of cholesterol decreases the death rate from all three diseases. Intake of 0 to 5 grams raises the probability of death for lung and colon cancer only. This question is probably best answered by recognizing that fact and eliminating those choices that include either lung or colon cancer.

16. **(G)** Standardizing the death rate involves correcting for variables inherent in the subject groups but not involved in the experiment. Age, weight, genetic histories, and accidental deaths are just some of the variables that the scientist must consider. However, (F) does not correct for intrinsic variables; rather, it ignores results that might not conform to a "neat" result. This does not standardize the death rate so much as "fudge" it. (H) involves an arbitrary assumption that is in fact incorrect. Assuming a zero death rate in the male population distorts the result of this experiment and does not correct for variations within the subject groups. (J) is incorrect because this experiment does not consider women at all. It might be valid to compare results with a different experiment involving women, but the actual death rates for men and women for different diseases are not necessarily similar (*e.g.*, the gender-related differences for breast cancer).

17. **(C)** Since voltage is directly related to current, voltage increases by the same factor as current if other variables are held constant. The same applies for resistance; therefore, the only correct formula is (C).

18. **(G)** $V = IR$, so the circuit with the greater resistance would have the greater voltage. Since resistance is directly proportional to resistivity, the germanium circuit would have the greater resistance and voltage.

19. **(A)** The total resistance R_s of the series resistors is $R_1 + R_2 = 2 + 2 = 4$. This resistance is double that of the circuit where $R = 2$. If R doubles, then the voltage doubles as long as the current remains the same.

20. **(J)** According to the formula for resistors in parallel: $\frac{1}{R_p} = \frac{1}{4} + \frac{1}{4} = \frac{2}{4} = \frac{1}{2} \Rightarrow R_p = 2$.

21. **(C)** If R is constant, then P increases with I^2; this is the definition of exponential growth.

22. **(J)** $V = IR \Rightarrow I = \frac{V}{R}$. To keep I constant if V increases, R must be increased.

23. **(D)** Compare Trials 2 and 3 to see what changing concentration of only one component has on rate. In this case, there is no change in rate with change in concentration of A, so rate is independent of concentration.

24. **(F)** Compare Trials 2 and 4, or Trials 1 and 3.

25. **(C)** Compare Trials 1 and 4, or Trials 2 and 3.

26. **(H)** Averaging or intermediate mechanisms do not work because one mechanism has no dependence on A with regard to rate. (G) is unlikely because a well-mixed solution should be homogeneous and have no pockets for mechanisms 1 and 2.

27. **(B)** This is a subtle question. (C) and (D) are incorrect because they over-generalize from a single case. It cannot be said that mechanisms can always be changed, (C), or that in every case the mechanism depends on solvent effects, (D). (A) is a special case of (D), where the claim is made that all reactions are solvent dependent. (B) alone allows for the possibility that solvents need not have an effect (note the word "may").

28. **(G)** acceleration $= \frac{D_v}{D_t} = \frac{\text{change in velocity}}{\text{change in time}}$.

    Experiment 1 (steel ball): The acceleration is constant at 3.50 m/sec^2. This can be demonstrated by choosing a time interval and dividing the corresponding velocity change during the time interval by the length of the time interval. For example, between 1 and 2 seconds, the velocity changes from 3.5 m/sec to 7 m/sec; therefore, acceleration equals $\frac{\Delta v}{\Delta t} = \frac{7 - 3.5}{2 - 1} = \frac{3.5}{1} = 3.5$ m/sec^2.
    For a time interval from 0.5 seconds to 1 second, the corresponding velocity would change from 1.75 m/sec to 3.5 m/sec; thus, the acceleration equals $\frac{\Delta v}{\Delta t} = \frac{3.5 - 1.75}{1 - 0.5} = \frac{1.75}{0.5} = 3.5$ m/sec^2.

    Experiment 2 (sled): The acceleration is a constant 4.9 m/sec^2. For example, the change in velocity corresponding to the time interval from 0.5 seconds to 1 second is 4.90 m/sec − 2.45 m/sec = 2.45 m/sec. The acceleration $= \frac{\Delta v}{\Delta t} = \frac{4.90 - 2.45}{1 - 0.5} = \frac{2.45}{0.5} = 4.9$ m/sec^2.
    Experiment 3 (box): The acceleration is constant at 0.66 m/sec^2.

29. **(A)** When friction is reduced in Experiment 4, the sled and the ball still travel at about the same accelerations as in the previous experiments. This can be demonstrated by using the equation $d = 0.5at^2$, which relates the distance that an object travels starting from rest to the time (traveling at constant acceleration) it takes to travel the indicated distance. Since the board is 10 meters in length, the distance that each travels is 10 meters.

    For the sled: $d = \frac{1}{2}at^2$
    $10 = \frac{1}{2}at(2.02)^2 \approx \frac{1}{2}(a)(4)$
    $a = 5$ m/sec^2
    For the ball: $d = \frac{1}{2}at^2$
    $10 = \frac{1}{2}a(2.39)^2 \approx \frac{1}{2}a(5.7)$
    $a = 3.50$ m/sec^2

    The ball and sled travel at about the same accelerations before and after oiling, so the differences in their relative accelerations must be due to something other than friction. The difference is the rolling of the ball.

30. **(H)** Experiment 4 shows that friction affects the relative acceleration between the box and either the sled or ball. Calculate the acceleration for the box: $d = \frac{1}{2}at^2 \Rightarrow 10 = \frac{1}{2}a(4.08)^2 \approx \frac{1}{2}a(16) \Rightarrow a = 1.25$ m/sec^2.
    Because the oiling in Experiment 4 caused a change in the box's acceleration, friction is a factor. Rolling must also be a factor as per the answer explanation to item #29.

31. **(B)** The acceleration of the ball is constant at 3.50 m/sec^2 (either Experiment 1 or 4). The acceleration of the sled is constant at 4.90 m/sec^2 (Experiment 2 or 4). Ratio $= \frac{3.50}{4.90} = \frac{5}{7}$.

32. **(H)** Although the acceleration of the ball is relatively insensitive to the amount of friction, the

ANSWERS AND EXPLANATIONS

acceleration of the box is very sensitive to friction. Therefore, in a ratio, the effect of changing the amount of friction will change the numerator (ball acceleration) only slightly, whereas the denominator (box acceleration) will change significantly depending on friction. (J) is not correct because the acceleration remains constant within each experiment.

33. **(B)** Two genetically distant species cannot breed.

34. **(H)** For early modern humans to completely replace Neanderthals, there could not have been a region containing Neanderthals that did not also contain early modern humans.

35. **(D)** Neither hypothesis necessarily rules out isolated communities. Both are concerned about areas where contact occurred.

36. **(J)** This information suggests that early modern humans killed Neanderthals, which supports Scientist 2.

37. **(C)** This fact shows that even if two species can breed, they may not do so voluntarily. Scientist 2 can therefore use this case as an example of the fact that two genetically compatible but dissimilar-looking animals choose not to interbreed. (D) is not readily relevant because lions and tigers are brought together artificially. No one disputed the notion that animals can interbreed, so (A) does not enter the argument. (B) is incorrect because lions and tigers do not share the same niche (tigers are solitary forest hunters while lions are group-hunting plains dwellers), and their ranges rarely overlap.

38. **(H)** The mixing of traits is part of Scientist 2's objections to Scientist 1's hypothesis.

39. **(A)** Both hypotheses attribute the disappearance of Neanderthals to early modern humans.

40. **(G)** (F) is a perfectly logical argument but it does not strengthen the position of Scientist 1. (J) does not strengthen the position of Scientist 1 since there is no way to prove from the given information whether others also died violently (clubs may have been used, or spearpoints that were used may have been valuable and were taken by the victors). Even if (J) is acceptable, it does not strengthen the position of Scientist 1. It only casts doubt on the position of Scientist 2. (H) is true in general. The only possible answer that strengthens a scientist's argument is (G).